Tree or Three?

An **elementary** pronunciation course

Ann Baker

CAMBRIDGE
UNIVERSITY PRESS

CAMBRIDGE UNIVERSITY PRESS

Cambridge, New York, Melbourne, Madrid, Cape Town, Singapore, São Paulo, Delhi

Cambridge University Press
The Edinburgh Building, Cambridge CB2 8RU, UK

www.cambridge. org
Information on this title: www.cambridge.org/9780521685269

First published 1982
Second edition 2006
3rd printing 2007

Printed in the United Kingdom at the University Press, Cambridge

A catalogue record for this publication is available from the British Library

ISBN 978-0-521-68526-9 paperback
ISBN 978-0-521-68527-6 paperback and audio CDs (3)

CONTENTS

ABOUT THIS BOOK

Who can use this book?

Tree or Three? is for beginner or elementary students who want to improve their English pronunciation. This book is for students working on their own, but teachers can also use many of the exercises in class. This symbol: 👥 means that an exercise is suitable for pairs. This symbol: 👥👥 means that an exercise is suitable for a group of students..

What do I need?

You need a CD player. Every time you see this symbol: 🎧 you have to listen to the CD. You will also see a number. This tells you which track number to find on your CD player. Intonation is shown with arrows: ⤴ ⤵

It is also useful to have a small mirror. You can use the mirror to compare the shape of your mouth with the mouth pictures in each unit.

Do I need to know any special vocabulary before I start?

Here is a list of some important vocabulary that will help you use the book. Check the words in a dictionary now and write a translation into your language below:

consonant . . . . tooth . . . .

lips . . . . teeth . . . .

mirror . . . . throat . . . .

nose . . . . tongue . . . .

pronunciation . . . . voice . . . .

sentence . . . . vowel . . . .

sound . . . . weak . . . .

strong . . . .

What do I have to do?

Each unit contains different exercises. Here is a list of some things you have to do:

listen to words and sentences on the CD

repeat words or sentences that you hear on the CD

tick words or sentences that you hear on the CD

underline words or letters

circle words or letters

match words that have the same sound

decide if information is **true** or **false**

Where can I check my answers to exercises?

For some exercises you will hear the answers on the CD after you speak.

For other exercises you will see this symbol: 🔑 This means you have to check your answers in the Key at the back of the book (see page 108–129).

Should I do all the units in the book?

You can look through the book and do any units that you feel are important for you.

If you want to check your pronunciation, it is a good idea to do all the units in the order that they appear in the book.

INTRODUCTION FOR TEACHERS

Level

This book is written for beginner–elementary students, but previous editions have also been used by students at other levels. *Ship or Sheep?* is written for intermediate level.

Class/Student working alone

The instructions are written for a student working alone, but can be used for classroom teaching as well. See the symbols in the section *About this book*, especially 🧍🧍 and 🧍🧍🧍.

Minimal pairs

In this book, these are pairs of words/sentences which differ by only one sound, e.g. *Have you got a pen?/Have you got a pan?* These sometimes help students to hear – and then pronounce – sounds that are difficult for them. You may want to extend students' class practice of particular minimal pairs by inventing games or playing the following:

- 'Card games' Make cards for all the minimal pairs in units 1–6. Shuffle the cards and deal them face down all around the table. Turn over any two cards and read the words aloud. If they aren't minimal pairs turn them face down again and the next person plays. Collect as many pairs as you can in a time limit, e.g. ten minutes.
- 'Fingers' For each pair, say words rapidly at random, e.g. *tree tree three three tree three*. Students show with one or two fingers if they hear sound 1 or sound 2. Students practise in pairs and then back to back.

Website support

More information and support for this book can be found at:
http://www.cambridge.org/elt/treeorthree/

THANKS AND ACKNOWLEDGEMENTS

In the preparation of this new edition I would like to thank:

Sally Mellersh (formerly of Hammersmith and West London College) for updating and expanding the *List of likely errors* to accompany the new editions of *Ship or Sheep?* and *Tree or Three?* by its inclusion on the website http://www.cambridge.org/elt/treeorthree/

David McCreath for IT assistance and contribution to my computer literacy. Sandra Turner for help with typing.

My editors Nóirín Burke, Frances Amrani and Roslyn Henderson, as well as the following teachers from all over the world who commented during development and gave me such practical advice:

Michele Chartrand-Hirsch, France; Ian Chitty, UK; David Deterding, Singapore; Sylvie Donna, UK; Elizabeth Downey, New Zealand; Lynda Edwards, UK; Laura Hancock, UK; David Hill, Australia; Kip Kelland, Italy; Kathy Keohane, UK; Andrea Paul, Australia; Gordon Francis Robinson, Singapore; Julietta Ann Schoenmann, UK; Roger Scott, UK

Continued thanks to J.D. O'Connor and Claude Boisson who advised me when planning order or presentation of sounds in the first edition of *Tree or Three?* Also Ralph Stanfield for his advice on student difficulties.

Illustrations by Johanna Boccardo, Pat Murray, Felicity House and Tony Wilkins

Cover design by Pentacor Book Design

Designed and typeset by Hart McLeod

UNIT 1 /s/ sun

1 Listen to /s/.
Look at the mouth picture.
Listen to /s/ and repeat.
You do not need your **voice**, just **air**.

2 Listen to the words and repeat:

1 **bus**

2 **glass**

3 **horse**

4 **house**

5 **bicycle**

6 **sofa**

7 **pencil**

8 **box**

9 **star**

10 **mouse**

11 **spoon**

12 **desk**

3 Listen to the questions and say the answers.

EXAMPLE: **What's number 1?**
Answer: **It's a bus.**

Pairwork
Ask a partner: 'What's number 1?',
'What's number 2? ...'

4 Look at the picture and listen to the conversation.

SARAH: What's this, Sam?
SAM: It's a bicycle.
SARAH: And what's this?
SAM: It's a house.
SARAH: What's this? A bus?
SAM: Yes.
SARAH: And what's this? A horse?
SAM: No, Sarah. It's a mouse!

5 Listen to the conversation again. <u>Underline</u> every /s/ sound.

EXAMPLE: Sarah: What'<u>s</u> thi<u>s</u>, <u>S</u>am?
Sam: It'<u>s</u> a bi<u>c</u>ycle.

6 Now listen to Sarah again. You are Sam. Practise the conversation.

EXAMPLE: Sarah: **What's this, Sam?**
Answer: **It's a bicycle.**

> **Pairwork**
> Practise with a partner:
> You are Sarah. Your partner is Sam.

7 Look at the pictures and listen to the sentences. Say new sentences.

EXAMPLE: **It's a cup**   Answer: **They're cups.**

ship

shop

hat

cat

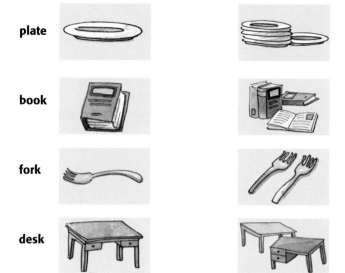

plate

book

fork

desk

8 Listen to the words. Put a tick ✓ if you can hear /s/ in the word.
Put a cross ✗ if you cannot hear /s/ in the word.

Example: pencil   ✓   picture   ✗

bicycle ▢   sofa   ▢

hat   ▢   answer   ▢

unit   ▢   listen   ▢

plate   ▢   conversation   ▢

UNIT 2 /z/ zoo

1 (A9) First say /s/ (see page 1).
Now listen to /z/.
Look at the mouth picture.

(A10) Listen to /s/ and /z/ and repeat.

Put your fingers on your **throat**.

Say /s/. What can you feel?
Say /z/. What can you feel?

You do not need your voice to say /s/.   /s/ is **unvoiced**.
You need your voice to say /z/.   /z/ is **voiced**.

2 (A11) Listen to the words and repeat:

SOUND 1	SOUND 2
/s/	/z/
Sue	zoo
bus	buzz
sip	zip
price	prize

3 (A12) Look at the pairs of sentences. Listen and tick ✓ the sentences you hear.

EXAMPLE: a) Look at that Sue! ▨   Look at that zoo! ✓

b) Listen to that bus. ▨   Listen to that buzz! ▨

c) Can I have a sip, please? ▨   Can I have a zip, please? ▨

d) It's a good price. ▨   It's a good prize. ▨

4 Look at the cartoon and listen to the conversation.

 Which words have /z/? <u>Underline</u> them.

Pairwork
Practise the conversation with a partner.

5 Look at the pictures and listen to the questions.

$/z/$ $/z/$
Answer: **Yes, it is.** or **No, it isn't. It's a ____.**

EXAMPLE: Picture 1: **Is this a horse?**
Answer: **No, it isn't. It's a cat.**

1 **horse** 2 **hat** 3 **star** 4 **book**

cat   plate   the sun   book

5 **cup** 6 **spoon** 7 **box**

glass   spoon   house

Pairwork
Ask your partner about the pictures: 'Is this a ...?'

6 A15 Look at the pictures and listen to the beginning of some sentences. Finish the sentences.

                     /z/   /z/

EXAMPLE: Picture 1: **These are flowers** …

                        /z/   /z/

Answer: … **and those are trees.**

> **Tip box**
> We say 'these' to talk about things which are near to us. We say 'those' to talk about things which are not very near.

1   trees / flowers
2   girls / boys
3   cows / dogs
4   cars / bicycles
5   windows / doors
6   planes / birds

7 A16 Listen to the words. Put them in the correct column.

isn't   sun   pens   is   buzz   bicycle   this
flowers   those   bus   boys   listen

/s/	/z/
EXAMPLE: sun	isn't

UNIT 3 /ə/ banana (1)

1   Listen to /ə/.
Look at the mouth picture.

  Listen to /ə/ and repeat.

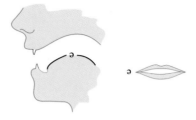

> **Tip box**
> Sometimes people say əəəə
> when they get up very early
> in the morning!

2   Look at the shopping list and listen to the words.
Part of each word is in **bold**. These parts are l-o-n-g and **strong**. They
are **stressed**.
Notice that /ə/ is never stressed. It is short and weak.

Shopping list

/ə/ pep**per**	/ə/ **butt**er
/ə/ /ə/ ba**nanas**	/ə/ **choco**late
/ə/ **pizza**	/ə/ **yog**hurt
/ə/ **carr**ots	/ə/ **news**paper

> **Tip box**
> /ə/ is the most common vowel sound in
> English. It is very short and weak and it
> helps to create the rhythm of English.

3   Now listen to the shopping list again and repeat.

Remember /ə/ is short and weak!

4 Look at the picture. Say what we need to buy.

EXAMPLE: **We need to buy a pizza, some butter and …**

> **Pairwork**
> Write your own shopping list. Read your list to your partner: 'I need to buy …'

5 A19 Listen to each group of words. Circle the word **without** /ə/.
We give the answer to Group 1.

Group 1	Group 2	Group 3	Group 4	Group 5
listen	horse	doctor	teacher	answer
banana	butter	question	hat	mother
cup	flower	window	pizza	shop

UNIT 4 /θ/ three

1 Listen to /θ/.
Look at the mouth picture.
 Listen to /θ/ and repeat.

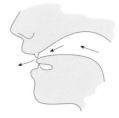

You do not need your **voice**, just **air**.   /θ/ is **unvoiced**.

2 A21 Listen to the words and repeat:

SOUND 1	SOUND 2
/s/	/θ/
mouse	mouth
sum	thumb
sick	thick
sink	think

3 A22 Look at the pairs of sentences. Listen and tick ✓ the sentences you hear.

EXAMPLE: a) Is that a mouse? ✓   Is that a mouth?

b) Look at this sum.   Look at this thumb.

c) It's sick.   It's thick.

d) It's sinking.   It's thinking.

4 A23 Listen to the words and repeat:

1st	first	6th	sixth
2nd	second	7th	seventh
3rd	third	8th	eighth
4th	fourth	9th	ninth
5th	fifth	10th	tenth

5 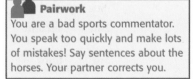 A24   Look at the pairs of words. Tick ✓ the words you hear.

EXAMPLE: a) seven ▨   seventh ✓

  b) three ▨   third ▨

  c) five ▨   fifth ▨

  d) eight ▨   eighth ▨

  e) ten ▨   tenth ▨

6 A25   Look at the picture and listen to some sentences.

Write T if the sentence is true. Write F if the sentence is false. Then check your answers.

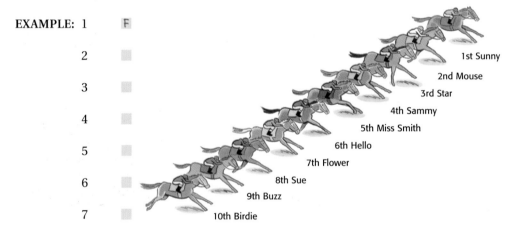

EXAMPLE: 1   F

  2   ▨

  3   ▨

  4   ▨

  5   ▨

  6   ▨

  7   ▨

1st Sunny
2nd Mouse
3rd Star
4th Sammy
5th Miss Smith
6th Hello
7th Flower
8th Sue
9th Buzz
10th Birdie

7   Imagine you work for a TV station. You are a sports commentator. Look at the picture of the horses again and say a sentence about each horse.

EXAMPLE:

Sunny is first. Mouse is second …

> **Pairwork**
> You are a bad sports commentator. You speak too quickly and make lots of mistakes! Say sentences about the horses. Your partner corrects you.

UNIT 5 /ð/ feather

1

 First say /θ/ (see page 9).

Now listen to /ð/.

Look at the mouth picture.

 Listen to /θ/ and /ð/ and repeat.

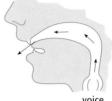

voice

 Put your fingers on your **throat**.

You do not need your voice to say /θ/.
You need your voice to say /ð/.

Say /θ/. What can you feel?
Say /ð/. What can you feel?
/θ/ is **unvoiced**.
/ð/ is **voiced**.

2   Listen to the words and repeat:

mother   **grandmother**   **father**   **grandfather**   **brother**

3   Look at the photograph of Sue's Family. Listen to Sue talking about her family.

This is my family. I'm in the middle, between my mother and my father. My big brother, James, is next to my father. My little brother, Peter, is next to my mother. And my grandmother and grandfather are here, behind us.

 Match the words with the people in the photograph.

Sue

Sue's mother

Sue's father

Sue's big brother, James

Sue's little brother, Peter

Sue's grandmother

Sue's grandfather

4 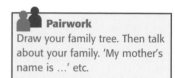 Read what Sue says again. <u>Underline</u> every /ð/ sound.

EXAMPLE: <u>Th</u>is is a picture of my family ...

Now read the text aloud. Remember /ð/!

5 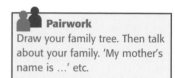 Look at Sue's family tree. Listen to some questions and answer, then listen to the answer given on the recording.

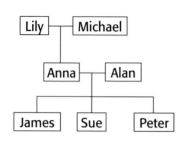

> **Pairwork**
> Draw your family tree. Then talk about your family. 'My mother's name is ...' etc.

EXAMPLE: **Who is Sue's mother?**
Answer: **Anna is Sue's mother.**

6 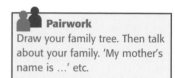 Listen to the words. Put them in the correct column.

mouth	fourth	these	father	thumb
feather	those	think	this	the

/θ/	/ð/

EXAMPLE:

/θ/	/ð/
mouth	these

UNIT 6 /iː/ sheep

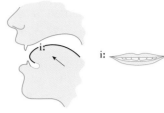

1 (A32) Listen to /iː/.
Look at the mouth picture.
(A32) Listen to /iː/ and repeat.
/iː/ is a l–o–n–g sound

2 (A33) Listen to the things on the menu
and repeat:

Tip box
When you see ː after a sound,
it means it is a l–o–n–g
sound

menu

café
Royal

Cheese sandwich................
Beef sandwich................
Ice cream................
Green tea................

3 (A34) Look at the picture and listen to the conversation.

A cheese
sandwich, please,
and a cup of
green tea.

1 cheese…
1 beef… 3 teas…
and 1 ice cream.

A beef sandwich,
please, and tea.

An ice cream for
me, please.

A cup of
green tea for
me, please.

4   (A34) Listen to the conversation again.
<u>Underline</u> every /iː/ sound.

Groupwork
Practise the conversation
with other students.

EXAMPLE: A ch<u>ee</u>se sandwich, pl<u>ea</u>se, and a cup of gr<u>ee</u>n t<u>ea</u>.

5 A35 Numbers and letters

Listen to the numbers and repeat:

3	13	4	14	5	15	6
16	7	17	8	18	9	19

6 A36 Listen to the letters and repeat:

b   c   d   e   g   p   t   v

7 Now spell these words:

cup   thirteen   sheep   tea

seventeen   cheese   eighteen   coffee

A37 Listen to the spellings and check.

Pairwork
You spell the words. Your
partner writes them down
and says them. You decide if
the spelling and pronunciation
are correct.

Tip box
To spell a word with two of the same
letters together, we can say 'double'.
E.g. book – 'B, double O, K'
coffee – 'C, O, double F, double E'.

UNIT 7 /ɪ/ ship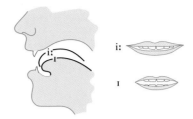

1

 First say /iː/ (see page 13).

 Now listen to /ɪ/.

Look at the mouth picture.

 Listen to /iː/ and /ɪ/ and repeat.

Say /iː/. Is it a l–o–n–g sound or a short sound?

Say /ɪ/. Is it a l–o–n–g sound or a short sound?

Tip box
When you see **:** after a sound, it means it is a l–o–n–g sound

2   Listen to the words and repeat:

	SOUND 1	SOUND 2	
	/iː/	/ɪ/	
	sheep	ship	
	bean	bin	
	meal	mill	
	heel	hill	

3   Look at the pairs of sentences. Listen and tick ✓ the sentences you hear.

EXAMPLE: a) Look at the sheep. ✓   Look at the ship. ▨

b) These are beans. ▨   These are bins. ▨

c) Is this a meal? ▨   Is this a mill? ▨

d) She likes high heels. ▨   She likes high hills. ▨

4   (A42)   Look at the pictures and listen to the beginning of the sentences.
Finish the sentences.

EXAMPLE: Picture 1: **It's a little** …
Answer: … **sheep**

1 **It's a little** ………   2 **It's a big** ………   3 **It's a big** ………   4 **It's a little** ………

5 **It's a big** ………   6 **It's a little** ………   7 **It's a little** ………   8 **It's a big** ………

5   Look at the pictures of the babies. Match the pictures with the adjectives.

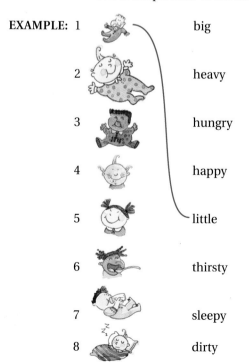

EXAMPLE: 1   big

2   heavy

3   hungry

4   happy

5   little

6   thirsty

7   sleepy

8   dirty

Listen to the adjectives and repeat.
Two adjectives have the sound /ɪ/. Which ones?
Now say a sentence about each picture.

EXAMPLE: Picture 1: **It's a little baby.**

6 Listen to the words and repeat:

horses   **boxes**   **sandwiches**   **faces**   **sixes**
glasses   **noses**   **buses**   **houses**

Do the all the words above end with /iːs/ or /ɪz/?

7 Look at the pictures and listen to the sentences. Say new sentences.

EXAMPLE: 1 **This is a box.**   Answer: **These are boxes.**

2 horse

3 glass

4 bus

5 face

6 nose

7 house

8 sandwich

UNIT 8 /f/ fish

1 (A46) Listen to /f/.
Look at the mouth picture.
(A46) Listen to /f/ and repeat.

You do not need your **voice**, just **air**. /f/ is **unvoiced**.

2 (A47) Listen to the words and repeat:

some flowers

four fish

a phone

a fly

a fire

Fred and Flora

a fork

some fruit

a knife

a leaf

the floor

3

1 There's a .... and a .... on the floor.

2 There's a .... next to the flowers.

3 There's some .... on the table.

4 There's a .... on Fred's head.

5 The four .... are in front of the fire.

(A48) Now listen and check your answers.

4 Listen to the sentences again and repeat.

5 Look at the picture again for 30 seconds.
Now cover the picture. What can you
remember?

 Pairwork
You describe the picture from
memory. Your partner looks at
the picture and corrects you.

6 ⌐ᴛ⌐   Match the words to the pictures:

EXAMPLE: 1 elephant

2 wife

3 office

4 phone

5 fire

6 laugh

7 photograph

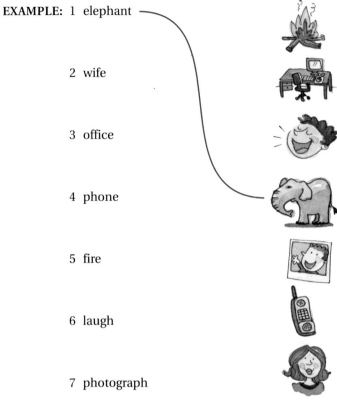

🎧 A49   Now listen to the words. <u>Underline</u> every /f/ sound.

EXAMPLE: ele<u>ph</u>ant

⌐ᴛ⌐   Look at the words again. How many ways can you spell /f/?

> 👥 **Pairwork**
>
> You spell the words. Your partner writes them down and says them. You decide if the pronunciation is correct.

UNIT 9 /v/ van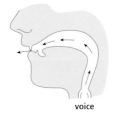

1

A50 First say /f/ (see page 18).
Now listen to /v/.
Look at the mouth picture.

A51 Listen to /f/ and /v/ and repeat.

voice

Put your fingers on your **throat**.

You do not need your voice to say /f/.
You need your voice to say /v/.

Say /f/. What can you feel?
Say /v/. What can you feel?
/f/ is **unvoiced**.
/v/ is **voiced**.

2 A52 Listen to the words and repeat:

Vincent   Vicky

five   seven

vase   twelve

3 Look at the sentences. <u>Underline</u> words with /f/ and (circle) words with /v/.
The first sentence is done for you:

<u>Fred</u> and <u>Flora</u> are (visitors.)

They are visiting Vincent and Vicky.

What have Vincent and Vicky got?

They've got a phone …

… and they've got some flowers.

Vincent   Vicky   Fred   Flora

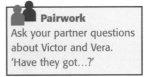

A53   Now listen to the sentences and repeat.

4   Look at the picture again. What else have Vincent and Vicky got?
Say six sentences.

EXAMPLE: **They've got some fruit …**
They've got …

5   A54   Look at the picture again and listen to the questions.
Answer: **Yes, they have.** or **No, they haven't.**

EXAMPLES:1 **Have they got a bowl of fruit?**
Answer: **Yes, they have.**

2 **Have they got five fish?**
Answer: **No. they haven't.**

> **Pairwork**
> Ask your partner questions
> about Victor and Vera.
> 'Have they got…?'

6   A55   Look at the pairs of words. Listen and tick ✓ the words that you hear.

EXAMPLE: a) ferry   ▨   very   ✓

b) van   ▨   fan   ▨

c) leaf   ▨   leave   ▨

d) fine   ▨   vine   ▨

e) view   ▨   few   ▨

UNIT 10 /w/ window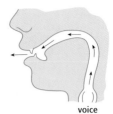

1   A56   Listen to /w/.
Look at the mouth picture.

 A56   Listen to /w/ and repeat.

voice

Put your fingers on your **throat**.
You need your voice to say /w/.

Say /w/. What can you feel? ?
/w/ is **voiced**.

> **Tip box**
> People sometimes say 'Wow!'
> when they are surprised

2   A57   Listen to the words and repeat:

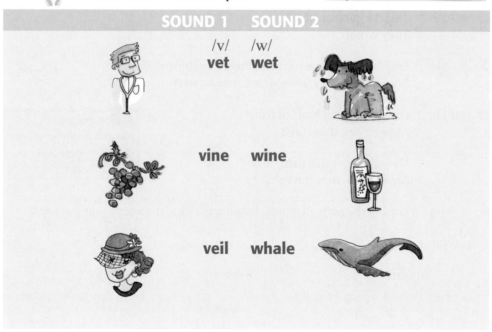

SOUND 1	SOUND 2
/v/	/w/
vet	**wet**
vine	**wine**
veil	**whale**

3   A58   Look at the pairs of sentences. Listen and tick ✓ the sentences you hear.

EXAMPLE: a) He's a vet student.　☐　　He's a wet student.　✓

b) There's a little vine here.　☐　　There's a little wine here.　☐

c) That's a veil.　☐　　That's a whale.　☐

4 Look at the picture, listen and repeat:
What's the weather like today?

It's warm in the north …

It's wet in the west…

It's windy in the east…

And it's snowy in the south!

5 Look at the picture again. Listen to some questions and answer:

'It's wet' **or** 'It's warm' **or** 'It's windy' **or** 'It's snowy'

EXAMPLE: 1: **What's the weather like in the north today?**
Answer: **It's warm.**

> **Groupwork**
> Ask other students about the weather in their countries or home towns: 'What's the weather like in …?'

6 Look at the cartoon and listen to the conversation:

What's the time?

It's quarter past twelve.

Excuse me! What's the time?

It's twenty past twelve.

What's the time, please?

It's quarter to one.

Excuse me! What time is it?

I'm sorry. I don't have a watch.

7 Listen to the conversation again. <u>Underline</u> every /w/ sound.

EXAMPLE: W<u>h</u>at's the time?
It's q<u>ua</u>rter past t<u>we</u>lve.

> **Groupwork**
> You are the man selling newspapers. Act out the conversation with other students.

8 Look at the clocks. What's the time?

EXAMPLE: 1. It's twelve o'clock

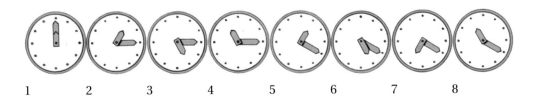

1   2   3   4   5   6   7   8

UNIT 11 /ə/ banana (2)

1   Say /ə/ (see page 7)

2 A62   Listen to the words.
Put a tick ✓ if you can hear /ə/ in the word.
Put a cross ✗ if you cannot hear /ə/ in the word.

EXAMPLE: flower ✓   coffee ✗

newspaper ▢   fruit ▢   the ▢   chocolate ▢

answer ▢   glass ▢   a ▢   vase ▢

3 A63   Look at the pictures, listen to the sentences and repeat.
Notice that /ə/ is never **stressed**, it is always weak.

EXAMPLE: 1
/ə/   /ə/   /ə/
It's a **glass** of **wat**er

2
/ə/   /ə/
It's a **cup** of **coff**ee

3
/ə/   /ə/
It's a **bowl** of **fruit**

4
/ə/   /ə/   /ə/
It's a **vase** of **flow**ers

5
/ə/   /ə/
It's a **news**paper

6
/ə/   /ə/   /ə/
It's a **piece** of **choc**olate

Look at the pictures again. Cover the sentences with a piece of paper. Say a sentence about each picture.
Remember /ə/ is weak!

4 Look at the cartoon and listen to the conversation.

5 Listen to the conversation again.
Every time you hear /ə/ write /ə/.

/ə/ /ə/

EXAMPLE: Anna: What's the time, Peter?

> **Pairwork**
> You are Anna. Your partner is Peter. Practise the conversation. Remember /ə/ is weak!

6 Look at the pictures and listen to some questions.
Answer: Yes, I **have**.' or 'No. I **have**n't.

EXAMPLE: 1 Have you got a mobile phone?
Answer: Yes, I **have**. / No, I **have**n't.

2   3   4

5  6   7

8  9   10

11   12

> **Groupwork**
> Ask the questions to other students: 'Have you got a ...?

Tip box
In the question 'have' is weak but in the answer 'have' is strong. This is because is it at the end of the sentence.

UNIT 12 /m/ mouth

1 A66 Listen to /m/.
Look at the mouth picture.
A66 Listen to /m/ and repeat.

voice

Put your fingers on your **throat**. Say /m/. What can you feel?
You need your voice to say /m/. /m/ is **voiced**.

2 A67 Listen to the words and repeat.

> **Tip box**
> People sometimes say
> 'Mmm' when they eat
> tasty food.

supermarket   swimming pool

farm   home

museum   cinema

3 A68 Look at the pictures and listen to the sentences.
Write T if the sentence is true. Write F if the sentence is false. Then check
your answers.

EXAMPLE: 1   There are three men in the supermarket.   F

2   There are two families in the cinema.

3   There is one woman at the farm.

4   The swimming pool is empty.

5   You can use your camera in the museum.

6   The woman is making dinner at home.

4   Look at the pictures again. Say correct sentences about each picture.

EXAMPLE: 1 There are two men and one woman in the supermarket.

> **Pairwork**
> Say sentences about the pictures. Your partner says 'true' or 'false' and corrects you when your sentence is false.

5 ⊶ A69   Listen to some words. Put a tick ✓ if you can hear /m/ in the word.
Put a cross ✗ if you cannot hear /m/ in the word.
Then check your answers.
Listen again and write the word in the space next to your answer

EXAMPLE:

1 ✓ .woman.........   2 ✗ ....answer......   3 ....

4 ....   5 ....   6 ....

7 ....   8 ....   9 ....

UNIT 13 /n/ nose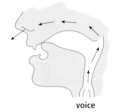

1 (A70) Listen to /n/.
Look at the mouth picture.
(A70) Listen to /n/ and repeat.

voice

Put your fingers on your **throat**.   Say /n/. What can you feel?
You need your voice to say /n/.   /n/ is **voiced**.

2 (A71) Listen to the words and repeat:

SOUND 1	SOUND 2
/m/	/n/
mice	nice
Tim	tin
mummy	money
mine	nine

3 (A72) Look at the pairs of sentences. Tick ✓ the sentences you hear.

EXAMPLE: a) These are mice.   These are nice. ✓

     b) That's my little Tim.   That's my little tin.

     c) That's her mummy.   That's her money.

     d) It's mine.   It's nine.

4 (A73) Listen to the numbers and repeat:

       1   9   10   15   16   18   19   21   29

5 Look at the clocks. Listen to the sentences and repeat:

 Nine o'clock in the morning.

One o'clock in the afternoon.

Ten o'clock in the evening.

Tip box
am = 'in the morning'
pm = 'in the afternoon'
Any time after 6pm = 'in the evening'

6 Now look at these clocks. What's the time?

EXAMPLE: 1 It's four o'clock in the morning.

2

3

4

Pairwork
Point at the clocks and
ask your partner:
'What's the time?'

7 Look at the cartoon and listen to the conversation.

8 Now listen to a similar conversation. Repeat each line.

Pairwork
Practise similar conversations with your partner.
Invite your partner to different places: the cinema,
the mountains, the supermarket, the moon!

UNIT 14 /ŋ/ ring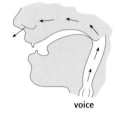

1   (A77)   Listen to /ŋ/.
Look at the mouth picture.

(A77)   Listen to /ŋ/ and repeat.

voice

Put your fingers on your **throat**.
You need your voice to say /ŋ/.

Say /ŋ/. What can you feel?
/ŋ/ is **voiced**.

2   (A78)   Listen to the words and repeat:

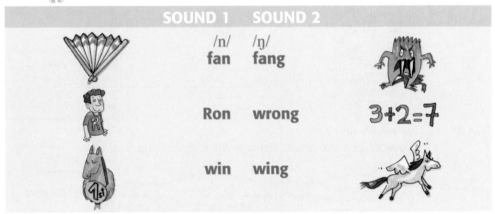

SOUND 1	SOUND 2
/n/	/ŋ/
fan	fang
Ron	wrong
win	wing

3 + 2 = 7

3   (A79)   Look at the pairs of sentences. Listen and tick ✓ the sentences you hear.

EXAMPLE: a) He's got two large fans.   ▨   He's got two large fangs.   ✓

   b) It's Ron.   ▨   It's wrong.   ▨

   c) It has two wins.   ▨   It has two wings.   ▨

4   (A80)   Listen to the words and phrases and repeat:

reading a book	**watching television**	**talking on the phone**
playing table tennis	**cooking a meal**	**brushing her hair**
sleeping	**eating an apple**	**drinking tea**

5

A81 Look at the picture and listen to some questions. Answer the questions using phrases from Exercise 4. Then listen to the answer given on the recording.

Pairwork
Ask your partner questions about the Long family: 'What's .... doing?'

EXAMPLE: 1: **What's Ben doing?**
Answer: **He's reading a book and eating an apple.**

6 A82a Look at Mrs Long. She's on the phone to her friend, Tina.
Now listen to their conversation.

Tip box
Look at the arrows. 'wh' questions (what, where, when, who or how) normally go down at the end. Other questions normally go up at the end. Lists go up on all the items, but down on the last item.

TINA: Morning! How are you?
MRS LONG: Oh, hi Tina! I'm fine, thanks.
TINA: What are you doing?
MRS LONG: I'm cooking lunch.
TINA: And what are the children doing?
MRS LONG: Well, Ron and Dan are playing table tennis, Ben is reading and Anne is washing her hair.
TINA: And is your husband washing the car this morning?
MRS LONG: No, he isn't! He's sleeping! What are you doing, Tina?
TINA: I'm talking to you on the phone!

7 A82b Now listen to Tina again. You are Mrs Long. Practise the conversation.

EXAMPLE: Tina: **Morning! How are you?**
Answer: **Oh, hi Tina! I'm fine thanks.**

Pairwork
Practise with a partner. You are Tina. Your partner is Mrs Long.

UNIT 15 /e/ pen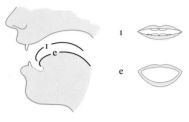

1
A83   First say /ɪ/ (see page 15)
Now listen to /e/.
Look at the mouth picture.
A84   Listen to /ɪ/ and /e/ and repeat.

2   A85   Listen to the words and repeat:

	SOUND 1	SOUND 2	
	/ɪ/	/e/	
	pin	**pen**	
	bin	**Ben**	
	tin	**ten**	
	bill	**bell**	

3 A86   Look at the pairs of sentences below.
Listen and tick ✓ the sentences you hear.

EXAMPLE: a) Have you got a pin?　▦　　Have you got a pen?　✓

b) That's my bin.　▦　　That's my Ben.　▦

c) That tin is very small.　▦　　That ten is very small.　▦

d) Can I have the bill?　▦　　Can I have the bell?　▦

4   A87   Listen to the words and repeat:

Ben	**Emma**	**clever**	**better**
Fred	**Jennie**	**very clever**	**best**

5 (A88) Look at the picture. Listen to the sentences and repeat.

Ben, Jennie, Emma and Fred are very clever.

Ben is a very good student.   Emma is better than Jennie.
Jennie is better than Ben.   Fred is the best student.

6 (A89) Now look at the pictures again and listen to some sentences.

Write T if the sentence is true. Write F if the sentence is false. Then check your answers.

Example: 1 F   4

           2   5

           3

> **Pairwork**
> Say sentences about the students in the picture. Your partner says 'true' or 'false' and corrects you when your sentence is false.

7 (A90) Listen to the letters and repeat:

f   s   x   l   m   n

8 Now spell these words out loud:

left   **lesson**   **boxes**   **next**

listen   **men**   **money**   **funny**

(A91) Listen to the spellings and check.

> **Pairwork**
> You spell the words. Your partner writes them down and says them. You decide if the pronunciation is correct.

9 (A92) Listen to each group of words. (Circle) the word **without** /e/.
The answer to Group 1 has been done for you.

Group 1	Group 2	Group 3	Group 4	Group 5
red	better	cinema	pen	exercise
apple	egg	bell	man	second
clever	banana	television	men	tea

UNIT 16 /æ/ man

1
(A93) First say /e/ (see page 32)
Now listen to /æ/.
Look at the mouth picture.
(A94) Listen to /e/ and /æ/ and repeat.

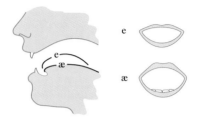

2 (A95) Listen to the letters or words and repeat:

	SOUND 1	SOUND 2	
	/e/	/æ/	
N	N	Anne	
X	X	axe	
	pen	pan	
	men	man	

3 🔑 (A96) Look at the pairs of sentences . Listen and tick ✓ the sentences you hear.

EXAMPLE: a) Her name is
Miss N. Smith. ▨   Her name is
Miss Anne Smith. ✓

  b) That's a very big X. ▨   That's a very big axe. ▨

  c) Have you got a pen? ▨   Have you got a pan? ▨

  d) The men lived here. ▨   The man lived here. ▨

4 Look at the picture. Listen to the sentences and repeat.

The Andrews Family

Grandfather Andrews

Grandmother Andrews

Karen Andrews   Max Andrews

Sally Andrews

Patrick Andrews

Max Andrews is very unhappy.
Karen Andrews is very happy.
Sally Andrews is carrying a bag.
Grandfather Andrews is wearing a hat.
Patrick Andrews is looking at the cat.
The cat is sleeping on the mat.

5 Listen to the sentences in Exercise 4 again. <u>Underline</u> every /æ/ sound.

EXAMPLE: M<u>a</u>x <u>A</u>ndrews is very unh<u>a</u>ppy.

6 Now look at the picture in Exercise 4 again but cover the sentences with your hand. What can you see in the picture?.

 Pairwork
You describe the picture. Your partner looks at the sentences and corrects you.

EXAMPLE: **Sally Andrews is carrying a bag.**

7 Listen to the words. Put them in the correct column.

pen	apple	and	second	pan	clever
men	better	grandfather		man	ten	cap

/e/	/æ/

EXAMPLE: pen   apple

UNIT 17 /ʌ/ cup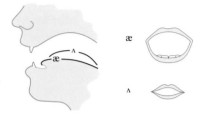

1

 First say /æ/ (see page 34)
 Now listen to /ʌ/.
Look at the mouth picture.
Listen to /æ/ and /ʌ/ and repeat.

2 B4 Listen to the words and repeat:

	SOUND 1	SOUND 2	
	/æ/	/ʌ/	
	cap	cup	
	hat	hut	
	cat	cut	
	fan	fun	

3 B5 Look at the pairs of sentences. Listen and tick ✓ the sentences you hear.

EXAMPLE: a) Is this your cap? ✓ Is this your cup?

b) Look at that little hat. Look at that little hut.

c) That's a very bad cat. That's a very bad cut.

d) It's a fan shop. It's a fun shop.

4 (B6)   Listen to the names and repeat:

Boys' names	Girls' names	Surnames
Sam	Anne	Love
Dan	Karen	Young
Jack	Patsy	London
Andrew	Sally	Mundy
Patrick	Hannah	

5 ⎯ (B6)   Look at and listen to the names again. Every time you hear /ʌ/ write /ʌ/.

EXAMPLE: /ʌ/
Love

6 (B7)   Listen to the words and repeat:

son   mother   brother   husband
uncle   cousin   grandson   grandmother

7 ⎯ (B7)   Listen to the words in Exercise 6 again. <u>Underline</u> every /ʌ/ sound.

EXAMPLE: s<u>o</u>n

8   Now look at this family tree:

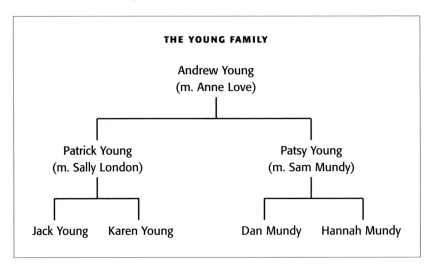

Choose the correct word to finish these sentences:

EXAMPLE: 1 Patsy Young is Dan Mundy's ......*mother*......   grandmother/mother.

2 Sam Mundy is Patsy Young's ....   husband/brother.

3 Dan Mundy is Sam Mundy's ....   son/brother.

4 Dan Mundy is Hannah Mundy's ....   uncle/brother.

5 Anne Love is Dan Mundy's ....   mother/grandmother.

6 Dan Mundy is Andrew Young's ....   grandson/son.

7 Patrick Young is Dan Mundy's ....   brother/uncle.

8 Jack and Karen Young are Dan's ....   uncles/cousins.

9 Sally London has just one ....   son/grandson.

10 Karen Young has just one ....   brother/cousin.

B8   Now listen, check and repeat the sentences.

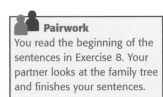
Pairwork
You read the beginning of the sentences in Exercise 8. Your partner looks at the family tree and finishes your sentences.

UNIT 18 /ɑː/ heart

1 (B9) Listen to /ɑː/.
Look at the mouth picture.

(B9) Listen to /ɑː/ and repeat.
Say /ɑː/. Is it a l–o–n–g sound or a
short sound?

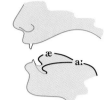

> **Tip box**
> When you see ː after a sound,
> it means it is a l–o–n–g
> sound.

2 (B10) Listen to the words and repeat:

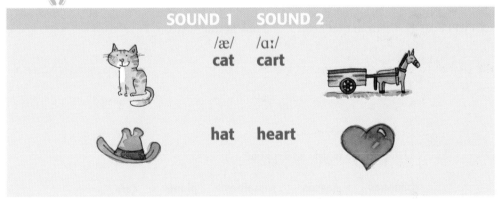

SOUND 1	SOUND 2
/æ/	/ɑː/
cat	cart
hat	heart

3 (B11) Listen to pairs of sentences. Write S if the sentences are the same.
Write D if the sentences are different.

EXAMPLE: a) D (I've got a little cat.   I've got a little cart.)

b)

c)

d)

4 B12 Listen to the words and repeat:

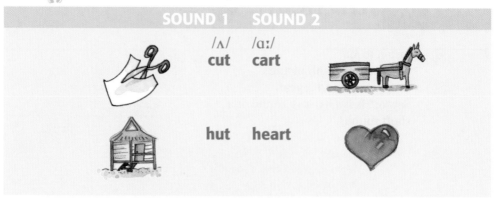

SOUND 1	SOUND 2
/ʌ/	/ɑː/
cut	cart
hut	heart

5 B13 Listen to pairs of sentences. Write S if the sentences are the same. Write D if the sentences are different.

EXAMPLE: a) S (Look at that heart.   Look at that heart.)

b)

c)

d)

6 B14 Listen to the words and repeat:

bananas   **glasses**   **tomatoes**   **plants**   **cars**
grass   **garden**   **are**   **aren't**

7 B14 Listen to the words again. <u>Underline</u> every /ɑː/ sound.

EXAMPLE: ban<u>a</u>nas

8 B15 Look at the picture and listen to some questions. Answer: **Yes, they are.** or **No, they aren't.**

EXAMPLE: 1: **Are the plants on the table?** Answer: **No, they aren't.**

 **Pairwork**
Ask your partner questions about the picture: 'Are the .... on the grass?', 'Are the .... on the table?'

UNIT 19 /h/ hat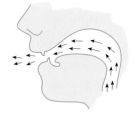

1 B16 Listen to /h/.
Look at the mouth picture.

B16 Listen to /h/ and repeat.

Put your fingers on your **throat**. Say /h/. What can you feel?
You do not need your voice to say /h/. /h/ is **unvoiced**.

2 B17 Listen to the words and repeat:

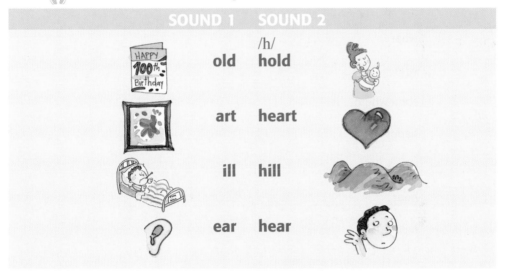

	SOUND 1	SOUND 2	
		/h/	
	old	hold	
	art	heart	
	ill	hill	
	ear	hear	

3 B18 Look at the pictures, listen and repeat:

1 **a horse**   **an elephant**   2 **a helicopter**   **an apple**

3 **a hat**   **an umbrella**   4 **a handbag**   **an orange**

4 Look at the pictures in Exercise 3 again and listen to some questions. Answer: **It's his.** or **It's hers.**

EXAMPLE: 1. **Whose horse is this?**
Answer: **It's his.**

5 All these words have 'h' in the spelling, but do we pronounce it?

 Listen to the words. Put a tick ✓ if you can hear /h/ in the word. Put a cross ✗ if you cannot hear /h/ in the word.

Pairwork
Ask your partner questions about the things in the pictures: 'Whose .... is this?' Then ask questions about things in your classroom: 'Whose pen is this?', 'Whose book is that?'

EXAMPLE: hotel ✓

honest ✗

what

who

somewhere

happy

when

hour

hello

Now check your answers.

6 Now listen again to the words with 'silent h' from exercise 5. Repeat them.

Pairwork
Say the words with a 'silent h' to your partner. Your partner writes them and says them. You decide if the spelling and pronunciation are correct.

UNIT 20 /ɒ/ clock

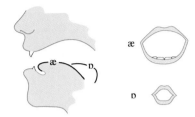

1 B22 Listen to /ɒ/.
Look at the mouth picture.
B22 Listen to /ɒ/ and repeat.

2 B23 Listen to the words and repeat:

SOUND 1	SOUND 2

/æ/	/ɒ/
cat	cot
Pat	pot
sack	sock
rack	rock

3 B24 Look at the pairs of sentences. Listen and tick ✓ the sentences you hear.

EXAMPLE: a) I want a white cat, please.   I want a white cot, please.

b) That Pat is very old.   That pot is very old.

c) There's a sack on the floor.   There's a sock on the floor.

d) Put it on the rack.   Put it on the rock.

4 B25 Listen to the words and repeat:

Sound 1	Sound 2	Sound 3	Sound 4
hat	hot	hut	heart
cat	cot	cut	cart

Now match the sounds to the correct symbol.

EXAMPLE:

Sound 1	Sound 2	Sound 3	Sound 4
/ɑː/	/æ/	/ɒ/	/ʌ/
(Unit 18)	(Unit 16)	(this Unit)	(Unit 17)

Which sound is a l–o–n–g sound?

5 B26 Look at the picture.
Then read the questions and match them to the answers.

EXAMPLE: a) What have they got in the first shop?   A lot of boxes.

    b) What have they got in the second shop?   A lot of clocks.

    c) What have they got in the third shop?   A lot of pots.

    d) What have they got in the fourth shop?   A lot of watches.

Now listen to the questions and answer, then listen to the answer given in the recording.

EXAMPLE: a): **What have they got in the first shop?**
Answer: **A lot of clocks.**

> **Pairwork**
> Ask your partner questions a)–d).

6 B27 Listen to a conversation in the fourth shop.

CUSTOMER: Have you got any boxes?
SHOP ASSISTANT: Yes, We've got a lot of boxes.
CUSTOMER: I want a very strong box, please.

7 B27 Listen to the conversation again. Underline every /ɒ/ sound.

EXAMPLE: Have you g<u>o</u>t any b<u>o</u>xes?

> **Pairwork**
> You are a shop assistant. Your partner is a customer. Practise four conversations: one conversation in each shop.

UNIT 21 /ɔː/ ball

1

B28 First say /ɒ/ (see page 43).
Now listen to /ɔː/
Look at the mouth picture.

B29 Listen to /ɒ/ and /ɔː/ and repeat.
Say /ɒ/. Is it a l–o–n–g sound or a short sound?
Say /ɔː/. Is it a l–o–n–g sound or a short sound?

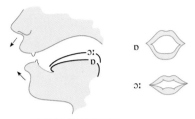

Tip box
Remember, when you see : after a sound, it means it is a l–o–n–g sound.

2 B30 Listen to the words and repeat:

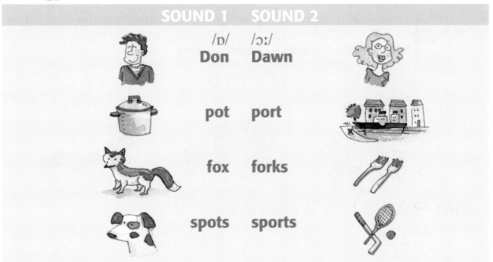

	SOUND 1	SOUND 2	
	/ɒ/	/ɔː/	
	Don	Dawn	
	pot	port	
	fox	forks	
	spots	sports	

3 B31 Look at the pairs of sentences. Listen and tick ✓ the sentences you hear.

EXAMPLE: a) Is your name Don? ▨   Is your name Dawn? ✓

b) That's a very big pot. ▨   That's a very big port. ▨

c) We don't want the fox in here. ▨   We don't want the forks in here. ▨

d) What a lot of spots! ▨   What a lot of sports! ▨

4   Match the sentences to the pictures:

EXAMPLE: 1 It's a large ball.

2 It's a small ball.

3 It's a long fork.

4 It's a short fork.

5 He's a tall footballer.

6 He's a short footballer.

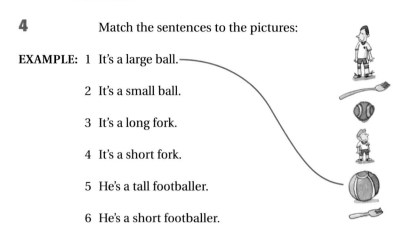

B32   Now listen to the sentences and repeat.

5   Look at the pictures. Say two sentences for each picture. Use these words:

tall   short   large   small   long

EXAMPLE: 1 **It's a tall doctor. It's a short doctor.**

6   Read the sentences and match them to the pictures:

1 It's a shop with four tall doctors in it.

2 It's a hut with four small foxes in it.

3 It's a long wall with a small door in it.

4 It's a bath with a lot of hot water in it.

Now listen to the sentences. <u>Underline</u> every /ɔː/ sound.

EXAMPLE: It's a shop with f<u>our</u> t<u>a</u>ll doctors in it.

7 Now try to draw a picture of …

… a long box with a lot of small balls in it.

… a large house with four small windows and a door.

… a tall glass with a little water in it.

> **Pairwork**
>
> Read the sentences in Exercises 6 and 7 to your partner. Your partner listens and draws pictures.

8 B34 Listen to the words. Put them in the correct column.

door	**watch**	**water**	**floor**	**sock**
stop	**call**	**rock**	**box**	**ball**

	/ɒ/	/ɔː/
EXAMPLE:	watch	door

UNIT 22 /ə/ banana (3)

1 Say /ə/ (see page 7)

2 Listen to the words and repeat:

/ə/
mother

/ə/
sister

/ə/
father

/ə/
grandmother

/ə/
brother

/ə/
grandfather

> **Tip box**
> Remember: /ə/ is the most common vowel sound in English. It is never l-o-n–g or **strong**. It is always short and weak.

3 Now listen to the phrases and repeat:

/ə/ /ə/   /ə/
mother and **fath**er

/ə/ /ə/   /ə/
brother and **sist**er

/ə/ /ə/   /ə/
grandmother and **grand**father

> **Tip box**
> We usually say mother like this: /mʌðə/ But the pronunciation changes when the next word begins with a vowel. We have to say /r/ at the end of mother: mʌðərənd … – See Unit 26.

4 Look at the picture. Sue is showing her photo album to Anna.
Anna is asking questions about the photos.
Listen to Anna's questions and repeat:

1 Is that your mother?

2 Is that your mother and father?

3 Is that your grandmother?

4 Is that your grandmother
and grandfather?

5 Is that your brother?

6 Is that your brother and sister?

5 Look at Sue's photos. You are Anna. Ask a question about each photo.

EXAMPLE: 1 **Is that your brother?**

1 2 3 4 5

6 7 8 9 10

> **Groupwork**
> Ask your group to show you
> photos of their families. Ask
> questions about the photos.

6 Listen to these sentences:

Question: **Can you sing?**
Answer: **Yes, I can.**

In the question 'can' is pronounced /kən/   This is the **weak** form.

In the answer 'can' is pronounced /kæn/   This is the **strong** form.
We use the strong form of
'can' when it is at the end
of the sentence.

7 Look at the pictures and listen to the questions. Practise answering with: **Yes, I can.**

Remember to say /kæn/ in the answer!

EXAMPLE: 1 **Can you see?**
Answer: **Yes, I can.**

1

see

2

walk

3

run

4

sing

5

read

6

swim

7

dance

8

use a computer

9

talk

Pairwork

Ask your partner the questions. Remember to say the weak form /kən/ in the question! Your partner says the strong form /kæn/ in the answer.

UNIT 23 /ɜː/ girl

1

 First say /ɔː/ (see page 45).
Now listen to /ɜː/.
Look at the mouth picture.
 Listen to /ɔː/ and /ɜː/ and repeat.
Say /ɔː/. Is it a l–o–n–g sound or a
short sound?
Say /ɜː/. Is it a l–o–n–g sound or a
short sound?

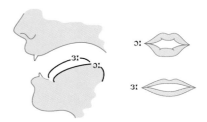

> **Tip box**
> Remember, when you see
> : after a sound, it means it
> is a l–o–n–g sound.

2 Listen to the words and repeat:

	SOUND 1	SOUND 2	
	/ɔː/	/ɜː/	
	Paul	**Pearl**	
	shorts	**shirts**	
	walk	**work**	
	board	**bird**	

3 Look at the pairs of sentences. Listen and tick ✓ the sentences you hear.

EXAMPLE: a) Is your name Paul? ✓ Is your name Pearl?

b) I want white shorts, please. I want white shirts, please.

c) He walks in the garden. He works in the garden.

d) It's a blackboard. It's a blackbird.

4   Read the phrases and match them to the pictures:

1 a bird and a worm

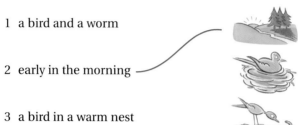

2 early in the morning

3 a bird in a warm nest

B44   Now listen to the phrases. <u>Underline</u> every /ɜː/ sound.

EXAMPLE: a b<u>i</u>rd and a w<u>o</u>rm

5   Read this proverb. What do you think it means?

THE EARLY BIRD CATCHES THE WORM

> **Groupwork**
> Do you have a proverb with a similar meaning in your language? Tell your group.

6   Look at the proverb again. How many /ɜː/ sounds are there? <u>Underline</u> them.
Now practise saying the proverb.

7   B45   Look at the pictures. Listen to the sentences and repeat:

1 Pearl gets up early to go to work.

2 Pearl's thirsty in the morning.

3 She puts on a shirt and a long skirt.

4 She walks to work at seven thirty.

5 Pearl arrives at work at eight thirty.

6 She's the first person at work.

Now look at the pictures again but cover the sentences. What does Pearl do every morning?

UNIT 24 /l/ letter

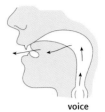

1

 First say /n/ (see page 28).
Now listen to /l/.
Look at the mouth picture.
 Listen to /n/ and /l/ and repeat.

voice

Put your fingers on your **throat**. Say /n/ and /l/. What can you feel?
You need your voice to say /n/ and /l/. /n/ and /l/ are **voiced**.

2 B48 Listen to the words and repeat:

	SOUND 1	SOUND
	/n/	/l/
	night	light
	nine	line
	Jennie	jelly
	bin	bill

3 B49 Look at the pairs of sentences. Tick ✓ the sentences you hear.

EXAMPLE: a) It's a lovely night.   It's a lovely light. ✓

b) Draw a nine.   Draw a line.

c) He loves Jennie.   He loves jelly.

d) Where is the bin?   Where is the bill?

4 B50 Look at the picture. Listen to the words and repeat:

a colour television

Ellen

a bottle of milk

a lemon jelly

a bowl of olives

a low table

a glass of lemonade

a slice of melon

a blue plate

Alan

a little animal

5 B51a Listen to Ellen talking to Alan.

ELLEN: Would you like some lunch, Alan?
ALAN: Yes please, Ellen.
ELLEN: A slice of melon?
ALAN: Yes please!
ELLEN: And a glass of lemonade?
ALAN: Yes please!
ELLEN: And some lemon jelly?
ALAN: Not now, Ellen. Maybe later!

Tip box
Look at the arrows. Ellen asks questions by making her voice go up at the end of the sentence. Practise this in the next exercise.

6 B52 Now listen to the conversation again. Repeat each line.

Pairwork
Practise the conversation. You are Ellen. Your partner is Alan.

7 All these words have 'l' in the spelling, but do we pronounce it?

B53 Listen to the words. Put a tick ✓ if you can hear /l/ in the word. Put a cross ✗ if you cannot hear /l/ in the word.

EXAMPLE:

yellow	✓	melon	
talk	✗	could	
television		bottle	
lovely		should	
half		folk	

Now check your answers.

8 8 Now listen again to the words with 'silent l' from exercise 7. Repeat them.

Pairwork
Say the words with a 'silent l' to your partner. Your partner writes them and says them. You decide if the spelling and pronunciation are correct.

UNIT 25 /r/ rain

1

B54 First say /l/ (see page 53).
Now listen to /r/.
Look at the mouth picture.

B55 Listen to /l/ and /r/ and repeat.

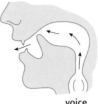

voice

Put your fingers on your **throat**.
You need your voice to say /l/ and /r/.

Say /l/ and /r/. What can you feel?
/l/ and /r/ are **voiced**.

2 B56 Listen to the words and repeat:

SOUND 1	SOUND 2

	/l/	/r/	
5+193+332	long	wrong	4+4=9 ✗
	light	right	3+3=6 ✓
	jelly	Jerry	
	glass	grass	

3 B57 Look at the pairs of sentences. Tick ✓ the sentences you hear.

EXAMPLE: a) It's a long sum.   ✓   It's a wrong sum.

b) It's light.   It's right.

c) Mary likes jelly.   Mary likes Jerry.

d) There's a flower in the glass.   There's a flower in the grass.

Tip box
Remember, sometimes we have 'silent letters' in English, e.g. the 'w' in 'wrong' is silent: /rɒŋ/.

4   B58   Look at the picture. Listen to the questions and answer.

EXAMPLE: 1: **Who's throwing a ball along the street?**
Answer: **Ros is.**

1 Who's throwing a ball along the street?

2 Who's dropping fruit along the street?

3 Who's watering trees along the street?

4 Who's driving a truck along the street?

5 Who's practising football along the street?

6 Who's drawing a line along the street?

> **Tip box**
> Look at the arrows. We ask 'wh' questions (who, what, where, when, how) by making the voice go down at the end of the sentence.

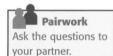

> **Pairwork**
> Ask the questions to your partner.

Now look at the picture again but cover the questions with a piece of paper. Say what you can see.

EXAMPLE: **Lara is drawing a line and Ros is throwing a ball.**

5   Look at some words from this unit:

grass	**street**	**truck**	**Fred**	**draw**
wrong	**tree**	**road**	**fruit**	**Patrick**

Underline the letter 'r' in all the words.

EXAMPLE: grass

What comes after 'r'?
A **vowel** sound or
a **consonant** sound?

> **Tip box**
> We always pronounce the letter 'r' when it comes before a **vowel** sound. When 'r' comes before a consonant sound, it sometimes becomes a 'silent r' – See Unit 26.

UNIT 26 'silent /r/' bird

1 Look at the words:

1 a horse
2 a bird
3 a girl
4 a carpet
5 a garden
6 a card

Underline the letter 'r' in all the words.

EXAMPLE: ho<u>r</u>se

 What comes after 'r'? A **vowel** sound or a **consonant** sound?

> **Tip box**
> In some English pronunciation (e.g. Australian and most British) 'r' is always silent before a **consonant** sound: bird = /bɜːd/. This is a 'silent r'. In other English pronunciation (e.g. American and Scottish), 'r' is always pronounced. bird = /bɜːrd/.

2 B59 Listen to a British person saying these words.

large   warm   thirsty   dirty

Is the letter 'r' pronounced or silent?

3 B60 Now listen to an American person saying these words.

large   warm   thirsty   dirty

Is the letter 'r' pronounced or silent?

4 B61 Now listen to some sentences describing the pictures in Exercise 1. Write B if the speaker is British. Write A if the speaker is American. The answers for Picture 1 and Picture 2 have been done for you.

Picture 1: It's a warm horse.   B   Picture 2: It's a thirsty bird.   A

Picture 3: She's a thirsty girl.   Picture 4: What a large carpet!

Picture 5: It's a very dirty garden!   Picture 6: It's a large card.

Now say the sentences. Do you prefer 'silent r' or pronounced /r/?

5 B62 Listen to the text and read. Is the speaker British or American?

THE WORST STUDENT
It's Thursday afternoon. Charlotte is
learning English and she's working hard.
She's learning thirteen words. But Charlotte
doesn't understand the first word!
She's the worst student in the world!

> **Tip box**
> Read the text. Every time you see
> r it comes before a **consonant**.
> This means you can choose:
> 'silent r' or pronounced /r/.

6 Do you understand these thirteen
words?

fourteen	**arm**	**thirty**	**yesterday**
forty	**dark**	**worse**	**exercise**
north	**party**	**hers**	**forget**	**important**

Say which words you understand and which words you do not
understand.

EXAMPLE: I understand the word 'arm'.
I don't understand the word 'north'.

> **Groupwork**
> Tell other students which
> words you understand.

7 B63 Look at the pictures. Listen to the phrases and repeat:

1 her pencils 2 /r/ her apples 3 her books 4 /r/ her eggs
5 /r/ her ice-creams 6 her flowers 7 /r/ her oranges 8 /r/ her umbrellas

Now look at the pictures again. Say a sentence about each picture.

REMEMBER: Sometimes you can choose 'silent r': r
Sometimes you must pronounce 'r': /r/

EXAMPLES: Picture 1: I can see four pencils.

Picture 2: I can see four /r/ apples.

> **Tip box**
> Remember, we have to pronounce the
> letter 'r' when it comes before a **vowel**
> sound e.g her apples. See Unit 25.

UNIT 27 /ɪə/ ear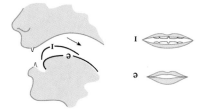

1

First say /iː/ (see page 13) and
then /ə/ (see page 7).

B64 Now listen to /ɪə/.
Look at the mouth picture.

B64 Listen to /ɪə/ and repeat.

> **Tip box**
> /ɪə/ is a **diphthong**. A diphthong is a 'double vowel': two vowels together.

2 B65 Listen to the words and repeat:

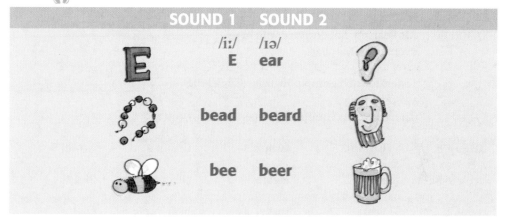

	SOUND 1	SOUND 2	
	/iː/	/ɪə/	
	E	ear	
	bead	beard	
	bee	beer	

3 🔑 B66 Look at the pairs of sentences. Listen and tick ✓ the sentences you hear.

EXAMPLE: a) A sheep's got two 'E's. ▨ A sheep's got two ears. ✓

b) He's got a bead. ▨ He's got a beard. ▨

c) That's a very big bee. ▨ That's a very big beer. ▨

4 B67 Look at the picture and listen to the conversation:

MR PEARSON: So, do you come here every year, Mr Lear?
MR LEAR: Oh yes, every year! I live near here, so it's very easy for me.
MR PEARSON: Well, I don't live very near so I can't be here every year.

5 ⚷— B67 Listen to the conversation again. <u>Underline</u> every /ɪə/ sound.

EXAMPLE: Mr Pearson: So, do you come h<u>ere</u> every y<u>ear</u>, Mr L<u>ear</u>?

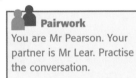

Pairwork
You are Mr Pearson. Your partner is Mr Lear. Practise the conversation.

6 B68 Listen to each group of words. (Circle) the word **with** /ɪə/.
The answer to Group 1 has been done for you.

Group 1	Group 2	Group 3	Group 4	Group 5
ice-cream	tea	clear	clean	idea
week	year	there	hear	chair
tear	bird	hill	Pearl	work

UNIT 28 /eə/ chair

1   First say /e/ (see page 32)
          and then /ə/ (see page 7).
 B69   Now listen to /eə/.
          Look at the mouth picture.
B69   Listen to /eə/ and repeat.

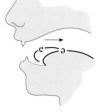

> **Tip box**
> /eə/ is a **diphthong**. A diphthong is a
> 'double vowel': two vowels together.

2   **B70**   Listen to the words and repeat:

	SOUND 1	SOUND 2	
	/ɪə/	/eə/	
	cheer	**chair**	
	pier	**pear**	
	here	**hair**	
clear	**clear**	**Claire**	

3 🔑 **B71**   Look at the pairs of sentences. Listen and tick ✓ the sentences you hear.

EXAMPLE: a) Three cheers!   ✓   Three chairs.   ▢

b) That's a big pier.   ▢   That's a big pear.   ▢

c) It's here – on the floor.   ▢   It's hair – on the floor.   ▢

d) Your name isn't clear.   ▢   Your name isn't Claire.   ▢

4   Look at the cartoon and listen to the conversation.

5  Listen to the conversation in Exercise 4 again.
Underline every /eə/ sound and (circle) every /ɪə/ sound.

EXAMPLE: Excuse me. Wh<u>ere</u>'s the <u>air</u>port? Is it n(ear)(here)?

> **Pairwork**
> Practise the conversation. Then have similar conversations about **the hairdresser's**
> and **the square**: 'Where's the hairdresser's?', 'Where's the square?' ...

6   Look at the picture and listen to some questions. Practise answering with:

Yes, there's a .... on the chair.
or **No, There isn't a .... on the chair.**

EXAMPLE: 1: **Is there a pen on the chair?**
Answer: **Yes, there's a pen on the chair.**

> **Pairwork**
> Ask your partner similar questions
> about the picture: 'Is there a
> .... on the chair?'

7 Listen to the words. Put them in the correct column.

idea	**chair**	**dear**	**beer**	**pair**
where	**Mary**	**here**	**disappear**	**square**

/ɪə/	/eə/

EXAMPLE:

/ɪə/	/eə/
idea	chair

UNIT 29 /ʊ/ book

1
 B75

 B76

First say /ɒ/ (see page 43)
Now listen to /ʊ/.
Look at the mouth picture.
Listen to /ɒ/ and /ʊ/ and repeat.

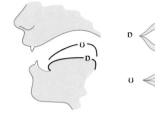

2 B77 Listen to the words and repeat:

SOUND 1	SOUND 2	
	/ɒ/	/ʊ/
	lock	look
	box	books
	rock	rook

3 B78 Look at the pairs of sentences. Listen and tick ✓ the sentences you hear.

EXAMPLE: a) I want a lock.　　✓　　I want a look.　　▢

    b) Give me the box, please.　▢　　Give me the books, please.　▢

    c) Look! A rock!　　▢　　Look! A rook!　　▢

4 B79 Look at the picture. Listen to the words and sentences and repeat:

The cooking pot is full.　　The cook is putting sugar in the cooking pot.

a cook

cookery books

a box of wood

Water is falling on the cook's foot.

5 🔊 ⓑ79   Listen to the words and sentences again. <u>Underline</u> every /ʊ/ sound.

EXAMPLE: c<u>oo</u>kery b<u>oo</u>ks

Look at the picture again for 30 seconds.
Now cover the picture. What can you remember?

> 👥 **Pairwork**
> You describe the picture from memory. Your partner
> looks at the picture and corrects you.

6   Look at the pictures. Say a sentence for each picture. Use 'push' and 'pull'.

EXAMPLE: Picture 1 **Look! He's pushing it.**
                Picture 2 **Look! He's pulling it.**

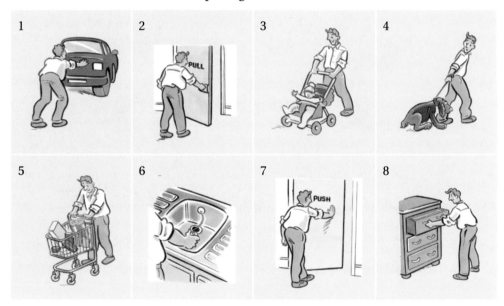

> 👥 **Pairwork**
> You point at a picture. Your partner says a sentence
> about it. You decide if the pronunciation is correct.

7 🔊 ⓑ80   Listen to the words. Put a tick ✓ if you can hear /ʊ/ in the word.
Put a cross ✗ if you cannot hear /ʊ/ in the word.

EXAMPLE: could ✓   shirt ✗

               wood ▨   girl ▨   full ▨   would ▨

               port ▨   foot ▨   sock ▨   good ▨

UNIT 30 /uː/ moon

1

B81　First say /ʊ/ (see page 63).
Now listen to /uː/.
Look at the mouth picture.

B82　Listen to /ʊ/ and /uː/ and repeat.
Say /ʊ/. Is it a l–o–n–g sound or
a short sound?
Say /uː/. Is it a l–o–n–g sound or
a short sound?

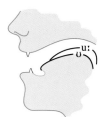

Tip box
Remember, when you see :
after a sound, it means it is
a l–o–n–g sound.

2　B83　Listen to the words and repeat:

SOUND 1	SOUND 2
/ʊ/	/uː/
pull	pool
look	Luke

3　B84　Listen to pairs of sentences. Write S if the sentences are the same.
Write D if the sentences are different.

EXAMPLE: a)　D　(It says 'pull' on this door.　　It says 'pool' on this door.)

　b)

　c)

　d)

4　B85　Listen to the words.

A	B	C
cooking	soup	good food
football	fruit	good schools
good books	blue shoes	cooking in the afternoon
sugar	swimming pools	looking at the moon

5 🔒 B85 Listen to the words in Exercise 4 again.
Write 'A', 'B', or 'C' to complete these sentences:

Column .... contains the sound /uː/.

Column .... contains the sounds /uː/ **and** /ʊ/.

Column .... contains the sound /ʊ/.

Now practise saying the words in columns A, B and C.

6 B86 Listen to the conversation and repeat:

JUNE: Do you like music?
SUE: Yes, I do.
JUNE: I like music too.

 Pairwork
Practise the conversation. Ask about music first and
then **everything** in Exercise 4, Columns A, B and C.
e.g: 'Do you like cooking?'

7 🔒 B87 Listen to the words. Put them in the correct column.

good	school	look	moon	pool
cook	tool	afternoon	foot	tooth

/ʊ/	/uː/
good	school

EXAMPLE:

UNIT 31 /t/ tin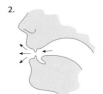

1 Listen to /t/.
Look at the mouth picture.

 Listen to /t/ and repeat.

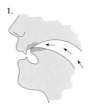

You do not need your **voice**, just **air**.   /t/ is **unvoiced**.

2   Listen to the words and repeat:

a telephone   a television   a teacup   a table

a letter   a teaspoon   a toy   a computer

Look at the pictures again. Use the word 'pretty' **or** the word 'dirty' to describe each picture.

EXAMPLES: Picture 1: **What a pretty telephone!**
Picture 2: **What a dirty television!**

> **Pairwork**
> You point at a picture. Your partner says a sentence about it. Talk about all the pictures.

3 Listen to the words and repeat:

1	a fat cat		fat cats
2	a wet hat		wet hats
3	a white shirt		white shirts
4	a hot plate		hot plates
5	a sweet biscuit		sweet biscuits
6	a quiet student		quiet students

4 B91 Look at the pictures in Exercise 3 again and listen to some sentences. Say new sentences.

EXAMPLE: Picture 1: **What a fat cat!**
Answer: **What fat cats!**

5 All these words have 't' in the spelling, but do we pronounce it?

B92 Listen to the words. Put a tick ✓ if you can hear /t/ in the word.
Put a cross ✗ if you cannot hear /t/ in the word.

EXAMPLE: time ✓

listen ✗

rest ▨

guitar ▨

castle ▨

night ▨

doctor ▨

whistle ▨

often ▨

> **Tip box**
> 'Often' can be pronounced in two ways:
> with /t/ or with 'silent t'

Now check your answers.

6 B93 Now listen again to the words with 'silent t' from exercise 5. Repeat them.

Pairwork
Say the words with a 'silent t' to your partner. Your partner writes them and says them. You decide if the spelling and pronunciation are correct.

UNIT 32 /d/ door

1

(C2)

(C3)

First say /t/ (see page 67).
Now listen to /d/.
Look at the mouth picture.
Listen to /t/ and /d/ and repeat.

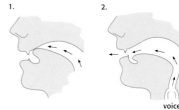

1.   2.

voice

Put your fingers on your **throat**.

You do not need your voice to say /t/.
You need your voice to say /d/.

Say /t/. What can you feel?
Say /d/. What can you feel?
/t/ is **unvoiced**.
/d/ is **voiced**.

2   (C4)   Listen to the words and repeat:

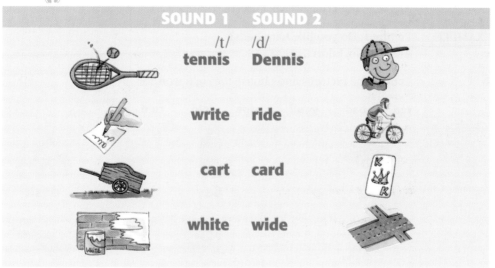

SOUND 1	SOUND 2
/t/	/d/
tennis	Dennis
write	ride
cart	card
white	wide

3 (C5)   Look at the pairs of sentences. Listen and tick ✓ the sentences you hear.

EXAMPLE: a) Do you like tennis? ✓   Do you like Dennis?

b) He can write well.   He can ride well.

c) That's a nice cart.   That's a nice card.

d) It's a white tie.   It's a wide tie.

4 (C6) Listen to the words and repeat:

cold   wide   old   hard

Now look at the pictures. Choose the correct word from the list above:

EXAMPLE:

1 a .... **bed**

2 a .... **wind**

3 an .... **friend**

4 a .... **road**

5 (C7) Look at the pictures again and listen to some questions.
Answer: '**Yes, I do.**' or '**No, I don't.**'

EXAMPLE: Picture 1: **Do you like hard beds?**
Answer: **No, I don't.**

> **Groupwork**
> Ask other students about the pictures in Exercise 4: 'Do you like ...?'

6 Look at the pictures and choose the right word:

red   bad   good   wide   old   cold

1 a .... **dog**	2 a .... **day**	3 a .... **desk**
4 a .... **doctor**	5 an .... **door**	6 a .... **dress**

(C8) Now listen and check your answers.

7 (C8) Listen to the phrases in Exercise 6 again and repeat.

> **Tip box**
> The /d/ at the end of the first word and the /d/ at the start of the second word **link** together. This means we only say the second /d/ /bædɒg/.

8 (C9) Look at the pairs of words. Listen and tick ✓ the words you hear.

EXAMPLE:

heart	✓	hard			hat		had	
town		down			coat		code	
try		dry			train		drain	

UNIT 33 /aʊ/ house

1
First say /æ/ (see page 34) and then /ʊ/ (see page 63).

C10 Now listen to /aʊ/.

Look at the mouth picture.

C10 Listen to /aʊ/ and repeat.

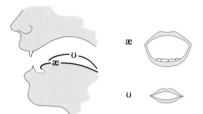

Tip box
/aʊ/ is a **diphthong**. A diphthong is a 'double vowel': two vowels together.

2 C11 Listen to the words and repeat:

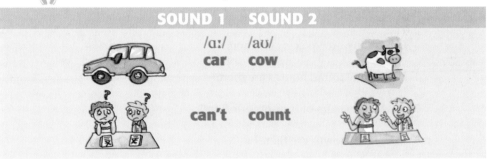

SOUND 1	SOUND 2
/ɑ:/	/aʊ/
car	cow
can't	count

3 C12 Listen to pairs of sentences. Write S if the sentences are the same. Write D if the sentences are different.

EXAMPLE: a) S (He's got a new car.   He's got a new car.)

b)

c)

d)

4 C13 Look at the picture. Listen to the words and repeat:

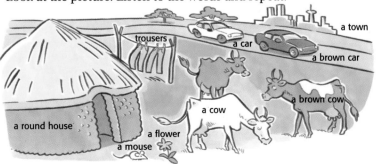

a town

trousers

a car

a brown car

a cow

a brown cow

a round house

a flower

a mouse

5 ⌂⊶ C13   Listen to the words again. <u>Underline</u> every /aʊ/ sound.

EXAMPLE: a r<u>ou</u>nd h<u>ou</u>se

6   C14   Look at the picture in Exercise 4 again. Listen to the questions below and answer, then listen to the answer given on the recording.
Start your answer with: '**There are….**' or '**There is…..**'

EXAMPLES: 1: **How many cows are there?**
Answer: **There are three cows.**

2: **How many flowers are there?**
Answer: **There is one flower.**

> **Tip box**
> We say: 'one mouse' (singular) and 'two mice' (plural). We do **not** say two mouses.

1 How many cows are there?

2 How many flowers are there?

3 How many brown cows are there?

4 How many round houses are there?

5 How many pairs of trousers are there?

6 How many towns are there?

7 How many brown cars are there?

> **Pairwork**
> Ask the questions to your partner.

8 How many mice are there?

7   Look at the picture in Exercise 4 again for 30 seconds.
Now cover the picture. What can you remember?
Say what you remember and try to draw the picture!

> **Pairwork**
> You describe the picture from memory. Your partner looks at the picture and corrects you.

UNIT 34 /əʊ/ phone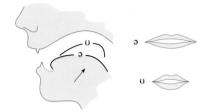

1   First say /ə/ (see page 7) and
then /ʊ/ (see page 63).

C15   Now listen to /əʊ/.
Look at the mouth picture.

C15   Listen to /əʊ/ and repeat.

> **Tip box**
> /əʊ/ is a **diphthong**. A diphthong is a
> 'double vowel': two vowels together.

2   C16   Listen to the words and repeat:

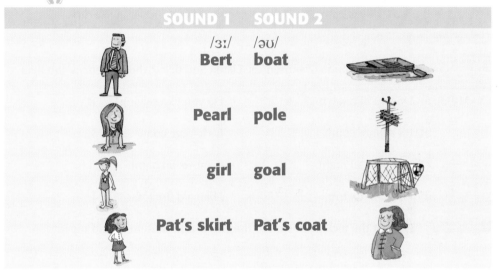

SOUND 1	SOUND 2
/ɜː/	/əʊ/
Bert	**boat**
Pearl	**pole**
girl	**goal**
Pat's skirt	**Pat's coat**

3   C17   Look at the pairs of sentences. Listen and tick ✓ the sentences you hear.

EXAMPLE: a) That's my Bert.   ▨   That's my boat.   ✓

b) There are two Pearls here.   ▨   There are two poles here.   ▨

c) What a fantastic girl!   ▨   What a fantastic goal!   ▨

d) Pat's skirt is very nice.   ▨   Pat's coat is very nice.   ▨

4 C18 Listen to the words and repeat:

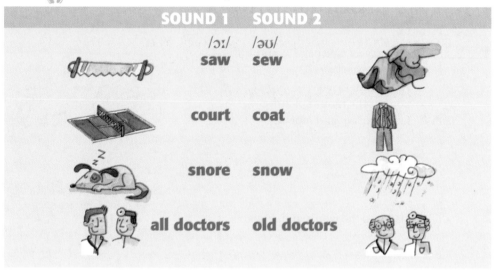

SOUND 1	SOUND 2
/ɔː/	/əʊ/
saw	sew
court	coat
snore	snow
all doctors	old doctors

5 C19 Look at the pairs of sentences. Listen and tick ✓ the sentences you hear.

EXAMPLE: a) Do you like sawing?   Do you like sewing? ✓

    b) It's a large court.   It's a large coat.

    c) It snores all night.   It snows all night.

    d) I like all doctors.   I like old doctors.

6 C20 Look at the picture. Listen to the words and sentences and repeat:

a cold nose

no coat

a warm coat

Joe's dog, Polo

cold toes

It's a cold morning.

It's snowing.

Joe is going for a walk with his dog, Polo.

7 (C21) Listen to the conversation:

ZOE: Hello Joe!

JOE: Hello Zoe!

ZOE: Where are you going? Are you going home?

JOE: No. I'm going to the mobile phone shop.

ZOE: Oh!

JOE: Where are you going? Are you going home?

ZOE: No. I'm going to the post office.

> **Tip box**
> The name Zoe is pronounced /ˈzəʊi/. Sometimes it is written like this: Zoë.

8 (C21) Listen to the conversation in Exercise 7 again. <u>Underline</u> every /əʊ/ sound.

EXAMPLE: Zoe: Hell<u>o</u> J<u>oe</u>!

Joe: Hell<u>o</u> Z<u>oe</u>!

> **Pairwork**
> You are Zoe. Your partner is Joe. Practise the conversation.

9 (C22) Listen to the words. Put a tick ✓ if you can hear /əʊ/ in the word. Put a cross ✗ if you cannot hear /əʊ/ in the word.

EXAMPLE: 1 know ✓

2 brown ✗

3 car

4 don't

5 October

6 work

7 nose

8 ball

9 mouse

10 joke

UNIT 35 linking /s/ this skirt

1   First say /s/ (see page 1)

2   C23   Listen to the words and repeat:

1	2	3	4
seat	**suit**	**skirt**	**stick**
5	6	7	8
spoon	**street**	**stamp**	**slipper**

3   C24   Now listen to the phrases and repeat:

this seat	this suit	this street	this spoon
whose seat	whose supper	his seat	Sam's supper

Tip box
The /s/ sound at the end of the first word and the /s/ sound at the start of the second word **link** together. This means we only say one /s/: this suit = /ðɪsuːt/.

4 C25 Listen to the conversation:

    SUE: Do you like this seat, Sally?

    SALLY: Yes. It's a nice seat, Sue.

    SUE: Whose seat is it?

    SALLY: It's Sam's seat.

> **Pairwork**
> You are Sue. Your partner is Sally. Practise similar conversations. Talk about all the pictures in Exercise 2.

5 C25 Listen to the conversation again and repeat each line. Remember 'linking s'!

6

Luke   Emma   Ben

Paul   Pete   Kate

C26 Look at the pictures. Listen to the questions below and answer, then listen to the answer given on the recording.

EXAMPLE: 1: **Who's sewing?**
      Answer: **Emma's sewing.**

  1 Who's sewing?

  2 Who's speaking to Sarah?

  3 Who's sleeping?

  4 Who's standing at the bus stop?

  5 Who's swimming?

  6 Who's studying?

> **Pairwork**
> Ask the questions to your partner.

UNIT 36 /ʃ/ shoe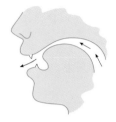

1

 First say /s/ (see page 1).
Now listen to /ʃ/.
Look at the mouth picture.
 Listen to /s/ and /ʃ/ and repeat.

Put your fingers on your **throat**.
You do not need your voice to
say /s/ and /ʃ/.

Say /s/ and /ʃ/. What can you feel?

/s/ and /ʃ/ are **unvoiced**.

> **Tip box**
> We sometimes say /ʃ/ 'Shhh!'
> when we want people to
> stop making noise.

2 Listen to the words and repeat:

	SOUND 1	SOUND 2	
	/s/	/ʃ/	
	sea	she	
	Sue	shoe	
	seat	sheet	
	sack	shack	

3 Look at the pairs of sentences. Listen and tick ✓ the sentences you hear.

EXAMPLE: a) Sea's very quiet today.   She's very quiet today. ✓

b) There are two Sues here.   There are two shoes here.

c) It's a clean seat.   It's a clean sheet.

d) What a dirty sack!   What a dirty shack!

4   Look at the pictures. Listen to the words and repeat:

1	2	3	4
England	**Sweden**	**Russia**	**Turkey**
Scottish	**Danish**	**Welsh**	**Polish**
English	**Swedish**	**Russian**	**Turkish**

5   Look at the pictures in Exercise 4 again. Listen to the questions below and answer, then listen to the answer given on the recording.

EXAMPLE: 1: **Is she Scottish or English?**
Answer: **She's English.**

1 Is she Scottish or English?   3 Is she Welsh or Russian?

2 Is she Danish or Swedish?   4 Is she Polish or Turkish?

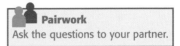
Pairwork
Ask the questions to your partner.

6 Match the words to the pictures:

EXAMPLE: **1** Russia

2 shoe

3 delicious

4 pronunciation

5 ocean

6 sugar

7 fashion

7 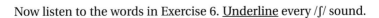 Now listen to the words in Exercise 6. Underline every /ʃ/ sound.

EXAMPLE: Ru<u>ss</u>ia

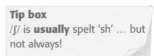
Tip box
/ʃ/ is **usually** spelt 'sh' ... but not always!

Look at the words again. How many ways can you spell /ʃ/?

UNIT 37 /ʒ/ television

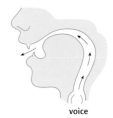

1

C34 First say /ʃ/ (see page 78).
Now listen to /ʒ/.
Look at the mouth picture.

C35 Listen to /ʃ/ and /ʒ/ and repeat.

voice

Put your fingers on your **throat**.

Say /ʃ/. What can you feel?
Say /ʒ/. What can you feel?

You do not need your voice to say /ʃ/.
You need your voice to say /ʒ/.

/ʃ/ is **unvoiced**.
/ʒ/ is **voiced**.

2 C36 Listen to the words and repeat:

usually   television   decision

3 Complete the sentences below with words from exercise 2.

SUE: Sarah, what do you ....*usually*.... do at the weekend?
SARAH: Well, I .... watch .... What do
you .... do, Sue?
SUE: Sometimes I go shopping and sometimes I watch ....,
too. It depends.
SARAH: I know. It's a difficult ....!

C37a Now listen to the conversation and check.

4 C37b Now listen to Sue again. You are Sarah. Practise the conversation.

EXAMPLE: Sue: **Sarah, what do you usually do at the weekend?**
Answer: **Well, I usually watch television. What do you usually do, Sue?**

Pairwork
Practise with a partner. You
are Sue. Your partner is Sarah.

5   Look at Sue's calendar.

Now read the questions and match them to the answers

1 What does Sue usually do on Saturdays?   She usually goes to the gym.

2 What does she usually do on Fridays?   She usually visits her grandparents.

3 What does she usually do on Sundays?   She usually watches television.

4 What does she usually do on Tuesdays?   She usually plays tennis.

5 What does she usually do on Thursdays?   She usually goes shopping.

6   C38 Now listen to the questions in Exercise 5 and answer them, then listen to the answer given on the recording

EXAMPLE: 1: **What does Sue usually do on Saturdays?**
Answer: **She usually goes shopping.**

> **Groupwork**
> Ask people in your group about their typical week: 'What do you usually do on ...?'

7   C39 Listen to the words. Put them in the correct column.

glass pleasure	shirt shower	measure garage	street push	shopping horse
/s/		/ʃ/		/ʒ/

EXAMPLE:

/s/	/ʃ/	/ʒ/
glass	shirt	measure

> **Tip box**
> Remember: /s/ and /ʃ/ are **unvoiced**, but /ʒ/ is **voiced**.

UNIT 38 /t ʃ/ chair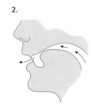

1

First say /t/ (see page 67) and
then /ʃ/ (see page 78).

 Now listen to /t ʃ/.
Look at the mouth picture.

 Listen to /t ʃ/ and repeat.

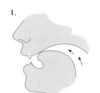

1.   2.

Tip box
/t ʃ/ is unvoiced.

2   Listen to the words and repeat:

SOUND 1	SOUND 2	
	/ʃ/	/t ʃ/	
	ships	chips	
	shop	chop	
	sheep	cheap	
	wash	watch	

3 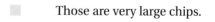 Look at the pairs of sentences. Listen and tick ✓ the sentences you hear.

EXAMPLE: a) Those are very large ships. ▨   Those are very large chips. ✓

　　　　　b) I don't like shopping. ▨   I don't like chopping. ▨

　　　　　c) That's a sheep farm. ▨   That's a cheap farm. ▨

　　　　　d) She's washing the television. ▨   She's watching the television. ▨

4 (C43) Look at the picture. Listen to the words and phrases and repeat:

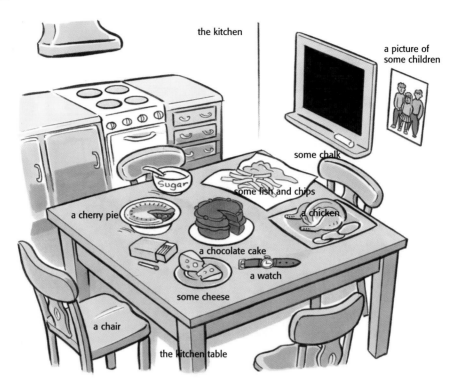

the kitchen

a picture of some children

some chalk

some fish and chips

Sugar

a cherry pie

a chicken

a chocolate cake

a watch

some cheese

a chair

the kitchen table

5 Look at the picture in Exercise 4 again.
What can you see *on* the kitchen table?
What can you see *near* the kitchen table?

EXAMPLES: **There's a watch on the kitchen table.**
There's a chair near the kitchen table.

6 Look at the picture in Exercise 4 again for 30 seconds.
Now cover the picture. What can you remember?
Say what you remember and try to draw the picture!

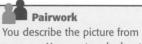

Pairwork
You describe the picture from memory. Your partner looks at the picture and corrects you.

7 Match the words to the pictures:

EXAMPLE: 1 question

2 cheese

3 watch

4 furniture

5 children

6 temperature

7 chess

8 picture

9 chin

10 future

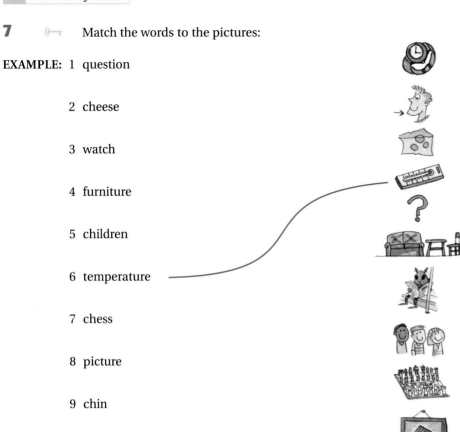

Now listen to the words. <u>Underline</u> every /tʃ/ sound.

EXAMPLE: ques<u>t</u>ion

8 Now put the words from exercise 7 in the correct column:

/tʃ/ is spelt **with** 'ch'	/tʃ/ is spelt **without** 'ch'
<u>ch</u>eese	ques<u>t</u>ion

EXAMPLE:

Tip box
/tʃ/ is **usually** spelt 'ch' ... but not always!

UNIT 39 /dʒ/ jam

1

C45

First say /tʃ/ (see page 82).
Now listen to /dʒ/.
Look at the mouth picture.

C46

Listen to /tʃ/ and /dʒ/ and repeat.

1.   2.

voice

Put your fingers on your **throat**.

Say /tʃ/. What can you feel?
Say /dʒ/. What can you feel?

You do not need your voice to say /tʃ/.
You need your voice to say /dʒ/.

/tʃ/ is **unvoiced**.
/dʒ/ is **voiced**.

2 C47 Listen to the words and repeat:

	SOUND 1	SOUND 2	
	/tʃ/	/dʒ/	
	cherry	Jerry	
	cheap	jeep	
	choke	joke	
	cheer	jeer	

3 C48 Look at the pairs of sentences. Listen and tick ✓ the sentences you hear.

EXAMPLE: a) Is your name Cherry? ▢   Is your name Jerry? ✓

b) I want a cheap type of car. ▢   I want a jeep type of car. ▢

c) I'm choking. ▢   I'm joking. ▢

d) The crowd is cheering. ▢   The crowd is jeering. ▢

4 (C49) Look at the picture. Listen to the phrases and repeat:

In the fridge **On the kitchen table**

chocolate cake

chicken

cherry pie cheese

German sausage

jelly

a jar of jam

oranges cabbage

Japanese noodles

vegetables

orange juice

5 (C49) Listen to the phrases in Exercise 4 again.
Complete the sentences below with /tʃ/ or /dʒ/.

1 Everything in the fridge contains the sound ....

2 Everything on the kitchen table contains the sound ....

6 (C50) Look at the picture in Exercise 4 again.
Listen to some questions and answer, then listen to the answer given on the recording.

EXAMPLES: 1: **Where are the oranges?**
Answer: **In the fridge.**

2: **Where's the chicken?**
Answer: **On the kitchen table.**

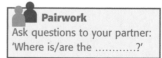

Pairwork
Ask questions to your partner:
'Where is/are the ....?'

7 Read and listen to the radio advertisement:

> A new shopping centre has opened in the city centre!
>
> You can buy Scottish jam and Irish cheese in 'The Farm
>
> House' or cheap fish and chips in 'Joe's Diner'. In 'Jerry's Place'
>
> you can also find delicious Japanese sushi.
>
> Oh and don't forget to visit 'Vegetable World' for the best
>
> fresh cabbage, spinach and carrots in town!
>
> Come to 'The Chessington Centre' tomorrow!

8 Listen to the advertisement again. Put the words in red in the correct column.

	/ʃ/ (Unit 36)	/tʃ/ (Unit 38)	/dʒ/ (this Unit)
EXAMPLE:	shopping	cheese	jam

Now try reading the advertisement aloud.
If possible, record yourself and listen.
Can you hear the difference between /ʃ/, /tʃ/ and /dʒ/?

UNIT 40 /j/ yoga

1 C52 Listen to /j/.
Look at the mouth picture.
C52 Listen to /j/ and repeat.

voice

Put your fingers on your **throat**.
You need your voice to say /j/.

Say /j/. What can you feel?
/j/ is **voiced**.

> **Tip box**
> The sound /j/ always comes
> before a vowel sound: you = /juː/,
> music = /mjuːzɪk/.

2 C53 Listen to the words and repeat:

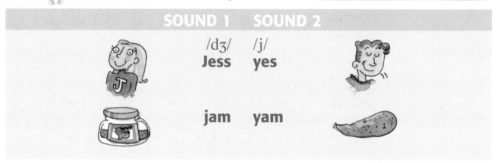

	SOUND 1	SOUND 2	
	/dʒ/	/j/	
	Jess	**yes**	
	jam	**yam**	

3 C54 Listen to pairs of sentences. Write S if the sentences are the same.
Write D if the sentences are different.

EXAMPLE: a) D (Jess, I love you!   Yes, I love you!)

b)

c)

d)

4

 Look at the picture of four friends. They are all very different.
Now listen to some information about the four friends (Yasmin /j/,
William /w/, Jemma /dʒ/, and Hugo /h/) and repeat:

 Look at the picture again. Who is Yasmin? Who is William? Who is Jemma?
Who is Hugo?
Write the names next to the people in the picture.

5 C56a Listen to an interview with Yasmin:

INTERVIEWER: **What's your name?**
YASMIN: **My name's Yasmin.**
INTERVIEWER: **And what do you do, Yasmin?**
YASMIN: **I'm a university student.**
INTERVIEWER: **What do you like?**
YASMIN: **Well, I like yoga and listening to music.**
INTERVIEWER: **And what do you hate?**
YASMIN: **Oh, I hate yoghurt and onions!**

6 C56b Now listen to the interviewer again. You are Yasmin. Practise the
conversation.

EXAMPLE: Interviewer: **What's your name?**
Answer: **My name's Yasmin.**

 Pairwork
Practise with a partner. You are the
interviewer. Your partner is Yasmin.
Then practise similar interviews
with William, Jemma and Hugo.

7 🎧 C57 Listen to each group of words. (Circle) the word **without** /j/.

The answer to Group 1 has been done for you.

Group 1	Group 2	Group 3	Group 4	Group 5
use	July	hello	Japan	new
year	onion	view	few	beautiful
(one)	uniform	student	music	jam

UNIT 41 /eɪ/ paper

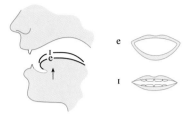

1

First say /e/ (see page 32) and
then /ɪ/ (see page 15).
Now listen to /eɪ/.
Look at the mouth picture.
Listen to /eɪ/ and repeat.

e

ɪ

Tip box
/eɪ/ is a **diphthong**. A diphthong
is a 'double vowel': two vowels
together.

2   Listen to the words and repeat:

	SOUND 1	SOUND 2	
	/e/	/eɪ/	
	pepper	paper	
	sell	sail	
	pen	pain	
	shed	shade	

3   Look at the pairs of sentences. Listen and tick ✓ the sentences you hear.

EXAMPLE: a) Pass me the pepper, please.   ✓   Pass me the paper, please.

   b) He's selling his boat.   He's sailing his boat.

   c) I've got a bad pen.   I've got a bad pain.

   d) It's cool in the shed.   It's cool in the shade.

4    C61   Look at the picture. Listen to the words and sentences and repeat:

the date
8 MAY
James
plates
a radio
a table
rain
a plane
Katy
Sadie
a train   a gate
a station
a railway
a baby
Jack
a newspaper

It's raining today.

James is making a cake.

Sadie and Katy are playing a game.

5   C62   Look at the picture in Exercise 4 again. Listen to the questions below and answer, then listen to the answer given on the recording.

EXAMPLE: 1: **What's James making?**
Answer: A cake.

1 What's James making?

2 What's Sadie playing with?

3 What's Katy playing with?

4 What's the baby playing with?

5 What's the date today?

6 Spell the baby's name.

7 Is the baby playing with pepper?

Pairwork
Ask the questions to your partner.

6   C63   Listen to the letters and repeat:

a   **h**   **j**   **k**

Pairwork
You spell the words. Your partner writes them down and says them. You decide if the spelling and pronunciation are correct.

7   Now spell these words out loud:

cake	**joke**	**Jack**	**hook**
jeep	**that**	**Katy**	**high**

C64   Listen to the spellings and check.

UNIT 42 /ɔɪ/ boy

1

First say /ɔː/ (see page 45) and
then /ɪ/ (see page 15).

 Now listen to /ɔɪ/.
Look at the mouth picture.

 Listen to /ɔɪ/ and repeat.

Tip box
/ɔɪ/ is a **diphthong**. A diphthong
is a 'double vowel': two vowels
together.

2 Listen to the words and repeat:

SOUND 1	SOUND 2	
	/iː/	/ɔɪ/	
	bee	boy	
	tea	toy	
	G	Joy	
	eel	oil	

3 C67   Look at the pairs of sentences. Listen and tick ✓ the sentences you hear.

EXAMPLE: a) Those bees are very noisy.　✓   Those boys are very noisy.

b) Let's go to the teashop.   Let's go to the toyshop.

c) Her name's Miss G. Smith.   Her name's Miss Joy Smith.

d) The eel is black.   The oil is black.

4 🎧 Match the phrases on the left to the pictures on the right:

EXAMPLE: 1 noisy boys

2 Lloyd's toys

3 a beautiful voice

4 boiling water

5 Joy's coins

6 enjoying oysters

7 engine oil

C68 Now listen to the phrases and repeat.

5 Look at these short conversations. Complete them with phrases from Exercise 4.

1 A: What do you need to make a cup of tea?
   B: You need a tea bag and some ......*boiling*......*water*............ .

2 A: That music is very loud.
   B: Yes, they're very ....

3 A: My car is making a strange noise.
   B: Maybe it needs some ....

4 A: She's a very good singer.
   B: Yes, she has a ....

5 A: Are these your toys?
   B: No, they're ....

Now listen and check your answers.

6 Now listen to the first part of each conversation in Exercise 5 again. Say the second part of each conversation.

EXAMPLE: 1. A: **What do you need to make a cup of tea?**
(You) B: **You need a tea bag and some boiling water.**

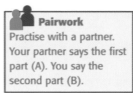

Pairwork
Practise with a partner.
Your partner says the first part (A). You say the second part (B).

UNIT 43 /aɪ/ kite

1

First say /ɑː/ (see page 39) and
then /ɪ/ (see page 15).

(C70) Now listen to /aɪ/.
Look at the mouth picture.

(C70) Listen to /aɪ/ and repeat.

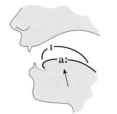

> **Tip box**
> /aɪ/ is a **diphthong**. A diphthong
> is a 'double vowel': two vowels
> together.

2 (C71) Listen to the letters and words and repeat:

SOUND 1	SOUND 2
/ɑː/	/aɪ/
R	I
bark	bike
cart	kite
guard	guide

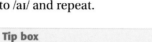

3 (C72) Look at the pairs of sentences. Listen and tick ✓ the sentences you hear.

EXAMPLE: a) His name's Mr. R. Smith. ▢   His name's Mr. I. Smith. ✓

b) What a noisy bark! ▢   What a noisy bike! ▢

c) That boy had a cart. ▢   That boy had a kite. ▢

d) My uncle is a guard. ▢   My uncle is a guide. ▢

4   C73   Listen to the phrases and repeat:

1 smiling	2 sunshine	3 driving
4 this exercise	5 climbing	6 riding
7 saying goodbye	8 flies	9 white mice
10 typing	11 ice cream	12 writing
13 ice-skating	14 flying kites	15 saying goodnight

5   Look at the phrases in Exercise 4 again.
Say what you like and what you don't like:

EXAMPLE: **I like driving but I don't like riding.**

Pairwork
Tell your partner what you like
and what you don't like.

6 C74 Listen to the conversation:

> MIKE: What are you doing tonight, Clive?
> CLIVE: I'm going ice-skating.
> MIKE: Have a nice time!
> CLIVE: Thanks. Bye!
> MIKE: Bye!

7 C74 Listen to the conversation in Exercise 6 again. <u>Underline</u> every /aɪ/ sound.

EXAMPLE: Mike: What are you doing ton<u>igh</u>t, Cl<u>i</u>ve?

> **Pairwork**
> You are Mike. Your partner is Clive. Practise the conversation.

8 C75 Listen to the words. Put them in the correct column.

garden **heart** **height** **start** **right**
fight **March** **bite** **artist** **inside**

/ɑː/	/aɪ/
garden	height

EXAMPLE:

UNIT 44 /p/ pen

1 C76 Listen to /p/.
Look at the mouth picture.

C76 Listen to /p/ and repeat.

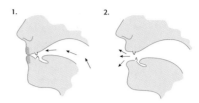

1. 2.

○— Put your fingers on your **throat**.   Say /p/. What can you feel?
You do not need your voice, just air.   /p/ is **unvoiced**.

2 C77 Look at the picture. Listen to the words and repeat:

The Paper Place   **Computer World**

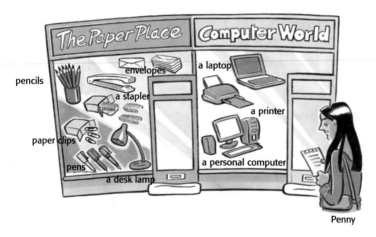

pencils

envelopes   a laptop

a stapler

a printer

paper clips

a personal computer

pens

a desk lamp

Penny

3 Penny starts university next week. Read her 'To do' list. Think how she will
ask for each of these things at Computer World.

> ## To do
>
> - repair my laptop
> - buy a new printer
> - buy a red pen
> - buy some staples and some paper clips

4   C78a   Now listen to a conversation in Computer World. Complete the sentences with words from Exercise 2.

PENNY: Hello, can I buy this ...printer........., please?
SALES ASSISTANT: No problem!
PENNY: And can you repair my ....?
SALES ASSISTANT: No problem!
PENNY: And can I buy ...., staples and ....
here?
SALES ASSISTANT: You can buy pens, ... and paperclips in The
Paper ...., next door.
PENNY: Thank you.
SALES ASSISTANT: No problem!

5   C78b   Listen to the conversation again and repeat each line.

> **Pairwork**
> You are Penny. Your partner is the Sales
> Assistant. Practise the conversation.

6   C79   All these words have 'p' in the spelling, but do we pronounce it?
Listen to the words. Put a tick ✓ if you can hear /p/ in the word.
Put a cross ✗ if you cannot hear /p/ in the word.

EXAMPLE: picture   ✓   photo   ✗

pepper   ▦   sheep   ▦

elephant   ▦   cup   ▦

Christopher   ▦   plate   ▦

headphones   ▦   phone   ▦

potato   ▦

Now check your answers.

7   C80   Now listen again to the words spelt with 'ph' in Exercise 6. Repeat them.

> **Tip box**
> When you see 'ph' in a word, it is
> pronounced /f/: elephant = /elɪfənt/
> philosophy = /fɪlɒsəfiː/.

> **Pairwork**
> Say the words with 'ph' to your
> partner. Your partner writes
> them and says them. You
> decide if the spelling and
> pronunciation are correct.

UNIT 45 /b/ book

1

(C81)

(C8)

First say /p/ (see page 99).
Now listen to /b/.
Look at the mouth picture.
Listen to /p/ and /b/ and repeat.

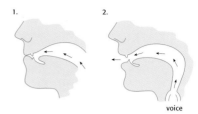

1.   2.

voice

Put your fingers on your **throat**.

Say /p/. What can you feel?
Say /b/. What can you feel?

You do not need your voice to say /p/.
You need your voice to say /b/.

/p/ is **unvoiced**.
/b/ is **voiced**.

2 (C83) Listen to the words and repeat:

SOUND 1	SOUND 2	
/p/	/b/	
pin	bin	
pear	bear	
pea	bee	
cap	cab	

3 (C84) Look at the pairs of sentences. Listen and tick ✓ the sentences you hear.

EXAMPLE: a) Have you got a pin?   ✓   Have you got a bin?

b) There's a pear in the tree.   There's a bear in the tree.

c) I don't like peas.   I don't like bees.

d) I want to get a cap.   I want to get a cab.

4 (C85) Listen to the words and repeat:

> **a black pen**   **a blue pen**   **a bottle of water**
> **a box of pencils**   **a rubber**   **a book**   **a bag**

5 (C86a) Look at the cartoon and listen to the conversation:

6 (C86b) Now listen to Bruce again. You are Penny. Practise the conversation.

EXAMPLE: Bruce: **Penny, what do I need for the biology exam?**
You: **You need a black pen, a blue pen, some pencils and a rubber.**

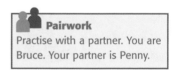

Pairwork
Practise with a partner. You are
Bruce. Your partner is Penny.

7   Match the words to the pictures:

EXAMPLE: 1 bread

2 plumber

3 thumb

4 banana

5 table

6 lamb

7 comb

8 bed

9 climb

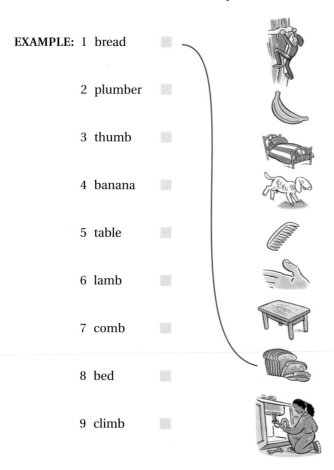

All the words have 'b' in the spelling, but do we pronounce it?
  Now listen to the words. Put a tick ✓ if you can hear /b/ in the word.
Put a cross ✗ if you cannot hear /b/ in the word.

EXAMPLE: bread   ✓   plumber   ✗

8   Now listen again to the words with 'silent b' in Exercise 7. Repeat them.

 Pairwork
Say the words with a 'silent b' to your partner. Your
partner writes them and says them. You decide if the
spelling and pronunciation are correct.

UNIT 46 /k/ key

1 (C89) Listen to /k/.
Look at the mouth picture.

(C89) Listen to /k/ and repeat.

1.   2.

Put your fingers on your **throat**.   Say /k/. What can you feel?
You do not need your **voice**, just **air**.   /k/ is **unvoiced**.

2 (C90) Look at the picture and listen to the conversation:

DOCTOR CLARK: Mr. Collins, how can I help you?
MR. COLLINS: Good morning, Doctor Clark. Can you cure my headache?
DOCTOR CLARK: Oh yes, I can cure it with acupuncture. Come back to the clinic at six o'clock.
MR. COLLINS: Thank you, Doctor Clark.
DOCTOR CLARK: Take care, Mr. Collins!

3 (C90) Listen to the conversation again. Underline every /k/ sound.

EXAMPLE: Mr. <u>C</u>ollins. How <u>c</u>an I help you?

> **Pairwork**
> Practise the conversation.

4   Look at these different ways to spell /k/:

'c'	'k'	'ck'	'ch'	'x' (the sound /ks/)
Doctor Clark	thank you	back	ache	six
acupuncture	take care	o'clock		
clinic				
cure				

Now look at some words. Put them in the correct columns above:

taxi   coat   milk   school   keep
cat   fix   lock   king   black

Pairwork
Say the words from Exercise 4 to your partner. Your partner writes them. Check the spelling together.

5   Match the sentences to the pictures:

EXAMPLE: 1 I can't walk because my knee hurts.

2 I need a knife to cut the bread.

3 My grandmother loves knitting.

4 I don't know the answer.

5 This doorknob is stuck.

6 There's a big knot in my shoelace.

Now listen to the sentences. Each sentence has a word with a 'silent k'. <u>Underline</u> it.

EXAMPLE: 1 I can't walk because my <u>knee</u> hurts.

Now check your answers.

6   Now listen again to the words with 'silent k' in Exercise 5. Repeat them.

Pairwork
Say the words with a 'silent k' to your partner. Your partner writes them and says them. You decide if the spelling and pronunciation are correct.

UNIT 47 /g/ girl

1 C93   First say /k/ (see page 104).
Now listen to /g/.

C94   Look at the mouth picture.
Listen to /k/ and /g/ and repeat.

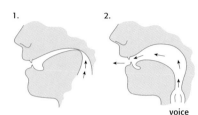

1.   2.

voice

Put your fingers on your **throat**.   Say /k/. What can you feel?
Say /g/. What can you feel?

You do not need your voice to say /k/.   /k/ is **unvoiced**.
You need your voice to say /g/.   /g/ is **voiced**.

2 C95   Listen to the words and repeat:

SOUND 1	SOUND 2	
/k/	/g/	
class	glass	
coat	goat	
curl	girl	
back	bag	

3 C96   Look at the pairs of sentences. Listen and tick ✓ the sentences you hear.

EXAMPLE: a) That's a very small class. ✓   That's a very small glass. ▨

b) I've got a white coat. ▨   I've got a white goat. ▨

c) What a lovely little curl! ▨   What a lovely little girl! ▨

d) There's something on
your back. ▨   There's something on
your bag. ▨

4 C97 Listen to the words and repeat:

1 dog	2 egg	3 fig	4 frog	5 wig
6 dogs	7 eggs	8 cakes	9 figs	10 books
11 frogs	12 clocks	13 wigs		

5 Look at the pictures in Exercise 4 again. Describe what Gabby likes and what Gabby doesn't like:

EXAMPLE: **Gabby likes dogs.**
Gabby doesn't like frogs.

6 C98 All the words below have the letter 'g', but do we pronounce it?
Listen to the words. Put a tick ✓ if you can hear /g/ in the word.
Put a cross ✗ if you cannot hear /g/ in the word.

EXAMPLE: eight ✗   ghost ✓   guess

angry   sign   gate

foreign   glue   fight

Now check your answers.

7 C99 Now listen again to the words with 'silent g' in Exercise 6. Repeat them.

Pairwork
Say the words with a 'silent g' to your partner. Your partner writes them and says them. You decide if the spelling and pronunciation are correct.

KEY

Unit 1

Exercise 5
SARAH: What's this, Sam?
SAM: It's a bicycle.
SARAH: And what's this?
SAM: It's a house.
SARAH: What's this? A bus?
SAM: Yes.
SARAH: And what's this? A horse?
SAM: No, Sarah. It's a mouse!

Exercise 8
pencil ✓   picture ✗   bicycle ✓   sofa ✓   hat ✗
answer ✓   unit ✗   listen ✓   plate ✗   conversation ✓

Unit 2

Exercise 1
When you say /s/ you cannot feel any movement in your throat: /s/ is unvoiced.
When you say /z/ you can feel movement (vibrations) in your throat: /z/ is voiced.

Exercise 3
a) Look at that zoo!
b) Listen to that bus!
c) Can I have a sip, please?
d) It's a good prize.

Exercise 4
VISITOR: Is this a box?
ARTIST: No, it isn't! It's a house.
VISITOR: Is this a house?
ARTIST: Yes, it is.
VISITOR: It isn't a house. It's a box!

Exercise 7

/s/			/z/			
sun	bicycle	this	isn't	pens	is	buzz
bus	listen		flowers	those	boys	

Unit 3

Exercise 5

Group 1	Group 2	Group 3	Group 4	Group 5
listen	(horse)	doctor	teacher	answer
banana	butter	question	(hat)	mother
(cup)	flower	(window)	pizza	(shop)

Unit 4

Exercise 3
a) Is that a mouse?
b) Look at this sum.
c) It's thick.
d) It's thinking.

Exercise 5
seventh   third   five   eighth   tenth

Exercise 6
1   Mouse is first.   F
2   Birdie is tenth.   T
3   Sammy is fourth.   T
4   Hello is third.   F
5   Buzz is ninth.   T
6   Miss Smith is eighth.   F
7   Flower is seventh.   T

Unit 5

Exercise 1
When you say /θ/ you cannot feel any movement in your throat: /θ/ is unvoiced.
When you say /ð/ you can feel movement (vibrations) in your throat: /ð/ is voiced.

Exercise 3

Sue

Sue's mother

Sue's little brother, Peter

Sue's grandmother

Sue's father

Sue's Sue's grandfather

Sue's big brother, James

Exercise 4

This is my family. I'm in the middle, between my mother and my father. My big brother, James, is next to my father. My little brother, Peter, is next to my mother. And my grandmother and grandfather are here, behind us.

Exercise 5

Anna is Sue's mother.
Alan is Sue's father.
James is Sue's big brother.
Lily is Sue's grandmother.
Peter is Sue's little brother.
Michael is Sue's grandfather.

Exercise 6

/θ/		/ð/		
mouth	fourth	these	father	feather
thumb	think	those	this	the

Unit 6

Exercise 4

FRIEND 1: A cheese sandwich, please, and a cup of green tea.
FRIEND 2: A beef sandwich, please, and tea.
FRIEND 3: A cup of green tea for me, please.
FRIEND 4: An ice cream for me, please.
WAITER 1: 1 cheese... 1 beef... 3 teas... and 1 ice cream

Unit 7

Exercise 3

a) Look at the sheep.
b) These are bins.
c) Is this a mill?
d) She likes high heels.

Exercise 4

1 sheep	2 ship	3 bin	4 bean
5 meal	6 mill	7 heel	8 hill

Exercise 5

'big' and 'little' have the sound /ɪ/: /bɪg/ /lɪtl/

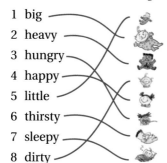

1 big
2 heavy
3 hungry
4 happy
5 little
6 thirsty
7 sleepy
8 dirty

Exercise 6

All the words in this exercise end with /ɪz/.

Unit 8

Exercise 6

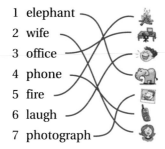

1 elephant
2 wife
3 office
4 phone
5 fire
6 laugh
7 photograph

You can spell /f/ in these ways:

'f'	'ff'	'ph'	'gh'
wi**f**e **f**ire	o**ff**ice	ele**ph**ant **ph**one **ph**otogra**ph**	lau**gh**

Here are more examples of words with these spellings:

'f'	'ff'	'ph'	'gh'
friend leaf	offer coffee stuff	physical graph	cough

Unit 9

Exercise 1
When you say /f/ you cannot feel any movement in your throat: /f/ is unvoiced.
When you say /v/ you can feel movement (vibrations) in your throat: /v/ is voiced.

Exercise 3
Fred and Flora are visitors
They are visiting Vincent and Vicky.
What have Vincent and Vicky got?
They've got a phone? ... and they've got some flowers.

Exercise 6
a) very   b) van   c) leave   d) fine   e) view

Unit 10

Exercise 1
When you say /w/ you can feel movement (vibrations) in your throat: /w/ is voiced.

Exercise 3
a) He's a wet student
b) There's a little vine here.
c) That's a whale.

Exercise 5
1 It's warm.   2 It's wet.   3 It's windy.   4 It's snowy.

Exercise 7
PEDESTRIAN 1: What's the time?
MAN SELLING NEWSPAPERS: It's quarter past twelve.
PEDESTRIAN 2: Excuse me! What's the time?
MAN SELLING NEWSPAPERS: It's twenty past twelve.
PEDESTRIAN 3: What's the time please?
MAN SELLING NEWSPAPERS: It's quarter to one.
PEDESTRIAN 4: Excuse me! What time is it?
MAN SELLING NEWSPAPERS: I'm sorry. I don't have a watch!

Exercise 8
1   It's twelve o'clock.
2   It's quarter past one.
3   It's quarter past five.
4   It's quarter past eleven.
5   It's twenty past one.
6   It's twenty past five.
7   It's twenty past seven.
8   It's twenty past eleven.

Unit 11

Exercise 2

/ə/ /ə/ /ə/
flower ✓   coffee ✗   newspaper ✓   fruit ✗   the ✓

/ə/ /ə/ /ə/
chocolate ✓   answer ✓   glass ✗   a ✓   vase ✗

Exercise 5

/ə/ /ə/
ANNA: What's the time, Peter?

/ə/
PETER: It's twelve o'clock.

/ə/ /ə/ /ə/ /ə/ /ə/
ANNA: Oh, and Peter, have you got a ruler?

/ə/
PETER: Yes, I have. Here you are, Anna.

/ə/ /ə/ /ə/
ANNA: Thanks. Have you got a calculator, too?

/ə/ /ə/
PETER: No, I haven't, Anna! Ask Emma.

Unit 12

Exercise 1

When you say /m/ you can feel movement (vibrations) in your throat: /m/ is voiced.

Exercise 3

1 F   2 F   3 T   4 F   5 F   6 T

Exercise 4

1   There are two men and one woman in the supermarket.
2   There are three families in the cinema.
3   There is one woman at the farm.
4   The swimming pool is full.
5   You cannot use your camera in the museum.
6   The woman is making dinner at home.

Exercise 5

1   woman   ✓
2   answer   ✗
3   mouse   ✓
4   banana   ✗
5   thumb   ✓
6   phone   ✗
7   camera   ✓
8   elephant   ✗
9   warm   ✓

Unit 13

Exercise 1
When you say /n/ you can feel movement (vibrations) in your throat: /n/ is voiced.

Exercise 3
a) These are nice.
b) That's my little tin.
c) That's her mummy.
d) It's mine.

Exercise 6
1   It's four o'clock in the morning.
2   It's nine o'clock in the evening.
3   It's ten o'clock in the morning.
4   It's three o'clock in the afternoon.

Unit 14

Exercise 1
When you say /ŋ/ you can feel movement (vibrations) in your throat: /ŋ/ is voiced.

Exercise 3
a) He's got two large fangs.
b) It's wrong.
c) It has two wins.

Exercise 5
1   He's reading a book and eating an apple.
2   She's brushing her hair.
3   He's sleeping.
4   She's watching television and drinking tea.
5   He's watching television.
6   She's talking on the phone and cooking a meal.
7   They're playing table tennis.

Unit 15

Exercise 3
a) Have you got a pen?
b) That's my Ben.
c) That ten is very small.
d) Can I have the bill?

Exercise 6

1	Ben is the best student.	F
2	Jennie is better than Ben.	T
3	Emma is better than Fred.	F
4	Jennie is better than Emma.	F
5	Fred is the best student.	T

Exercise 9

Group 1	Group 2	Group 3	Group 4	Group 5
red	better	(cinema)	pen	exercise
(apple)	egg	bell	(man)	second
clever	(banana)	television	men	(tea)

Unit 16

Exercise 3

a) Her name is Miss Anne Smith.
b) That's a very big X.
c) Have you got a pen?
d) The man lived here.

Exercise 5

Max Andrews is very unhappy.
Karen Andrews is very happy.
Sally Andrews is carrying a bag.
Grandfather Andrews is wearing a hat.
Patrick Andrews is looking at the cat.
The cat is sleeping on the mat.

Exercise 7

/e/			/æ/		
pen	second		apple	and	pan
clever	men		grandfather		
better	ten		man	cap	

Unit 17

Exercise 3
a) Is this your cap?
b) Look at that little hut.
c) That's a very bad cut.
d) It's a fun shop.

Exercise 5

/ʌ/	/ʌ/	/ʌ/	/ʌ/
Love	Young	London	Mundy

Exercise 7
s<u>o</u>n   m<u>o</u>ther   br<u>o</u>ther   h<u>u</u>sband
<u>u</u>ncle   c<u>ou</u>sin   grands<u>o</u>n   grandm<u>o</u>ther

Unit 18

Exercise 3
a) D   I've got a little cat.   I've got a little cart.
b) S   That's a lovely heart.   That's a lovely heart.
c) D   That's a lovely heart.   That's a lovely hat.
d) S   I've got a little cat.   I've got a little cat.

Exercise 5
a) S   Look at that heart.   Look at that heart.
b) D   That's a very bad cut.   That's a very bad cart.
c) D   Look at that hut.   Look at that heart.
d) S   That's a very bad cut.   That's a very bad cut.

Exercise 7
ban<u>a</u>nas   gl<u>a</u>sses   tom<u>a</u>toes   pl<u>a</u>nts   c<u>a</u>rs   gr<u>a</u>ss
g<u>a</u>rden   <u>a</u>re   <u>a</u>ren't

Exercise 8
1 No they aren't.
2 Yes they are.
3 Yes they are.
4 No they aren't.
5 Yes they are.
6 No they aren't.
7 Yes they are.

Unit 19

Exercise 1
When you say /h/ you cannot feel movement (vibrations) in your throat: /h/ is unvoiced.

Exercise 4

1 It's his.	2 It's hers.	3 It's his.	4 It's hers.
5 It's hers.	6 It's his.	7 It's hers.	8 It's hers.

Exercise 5

hotel ✓   honest ✗   what ✗   who ✓   somewhere ✗
happy ✓   when ✗   hour ✗   hello ✓

Unit 20

Exercise 3

a) I want a white cot, please.
b) That pot is very old.
c) There's a sock on the floor.
d) Put it on the rack.

Exercise 4

Sound 1: /æ/   Sound 2: /ɒ/   Sound 3: /ʌ/   Sound 4: /ɑː/   /ɑː/ is a l-o-n-g sound.

Exercise 5

a) A lot of clocks.   b) A lot of pots.   c) A lot of watches.   d) A lot of boxes.

Exercise 7

CUSTOMER: Have you got any b<u>o</u>xes?
SHOP ASSISTANT: Yes, We've g<u>o</u>t a l<u>o</u>t of b<u>o</u>xes.
CUSTOMER: I w<u>a</u>nt a very str<u>o</u>ng b<u>o</u>x, please.

Unit 21

Exercise 3

a) Is your name Dawn?
b) That's a very big pot.
c) We don't want the forks in here.
d) What a lot of spots!

Exercise 4

1 It's a large ball.
2 It's a small ball.
3 It's a long fork.
4 It's a short fork.
5 He's a tall footballer.
6 He's a short footballer.

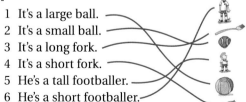

Exercise 5

1 It's a tall doctor. It's a short doctor.
2 It's a large box. It's a small box.
3 It's a long piece of chalk. It's a short piece of chalk.

Exercise 6

It's a shop with <u>fou</u>r <u>ta</u>ll doctors in it.
It's a hut with <u>fou</u>r sm<u>a</u>ll foxes in it.
It's a long w<u>a</u>ll with a sm<u>a</u>ll d<u>oo</u>r in it.
It's a bath with a lot of hot w<u>a</u>ter in it.

Exercise 8

/ɒ/			/ɔː/		
watch	sock	stop	door	water	floor
rock	box		call	ball	

Unit 22

Exercise 5

1 Is that your brother?
2 Is that your brother and sister?
3 Is that your grandmother?
4 Is that your grandmother and grandfather?
5 Is that your father?
6 Is that your brother and father?
7 Is that your sister?
8 Is that your sister and grandfather?
9 Is that your grandfather?
10 Is that your grandfather and father?

Unit 23

Exercise 3

a) Is your name Paul?
b) I want white shirts, please.
c) He walks in the garden.
d) It's a blackbird.

Exercise 4

a b<u>ir</u>d and a w<u>or</u>m
<u>ear</u>ly in the morning
a b<u>ir</u>d in a warm nest

Exercise 5
This proverb means if you start something early and do not waste time, you will probably be more successful.

Exercise 6
The <u>ea</u>rly <u>bir</u>d catches the w<u>or</u>m.

Unit 24

Exercise 1
Put your fingers on your throat:
When you say /n/ and /l/ you can feel movement (vibrations) in your throat:
/n/ and /l/ are voiced.

Exercise 3
a) It's a lovely light.
b) Draw a line.
c) He loves Jennie.
d) Where is the bin?

Exercise 7
yellow ✓   talk ✗   television ✓   lovely ✓   half ✗
melon ✓   could ✗   bottle ✓   should ✗   folk ✗

Unit 25

Exercise 1
When you say /l/ and /r/ you can feel movement (vibrations) in your throat:
/l/ and /r/ are voiced.

Exercise 3
a) It's a long sum.
b) It's right.
c) Mary likes jelly.
d) There's a flower in the grass.

Exercise 5
In these words, there is a **vowel** sound after the letter 'r'. This means we have to pronounce the letter 'r'. See the Tip box on page 56.

Unit 26

Exercise 1
In these words, there is a **consonant** sound after the letter 'r'. This means the letter 'r' is not always pronounced. See the Tip box on page 57.

Exercise 2
The letter 'r' is silent. This is common in Australian and most British English.

Exercise 3
The letter 'r' is pronounced. This is common in American and Scottish English.

Exercise 4
1 B   2 A   3 B   4 B   5 A   6 B

Exercise 5
The speaker is British.

Unit 27

Exercise 3
a) A sheep's got two ears.
b) He's got a beard.
c) That's a very big beer.

Exercise 5
MR. PEARSON: So, do you come h<u>ere</u> every y<u>ear</u>, Mr. L<u>ear</u>?
    MR. LEAR: Oh yes, every y<u>ear</u>! I live n<u>ear</u> h<u>ere</u>, so it's very easy for me.
MR. PEARSON: Well, I don't live very n<u>ear</u> so I can't be h<u>ere</u> every y<u>ear</u>.

Exercise 6

Group 1	Group 2	Group 3	Group 4	Group 5
ice-cream	tea	(clear)	clean	(idea)
week	(year)	there	(hear)	chair
(tear)	bird	hill	Pearl	work

Unit 28

Exercise 3
a) Three cheers!
b) That's a big pear.
c) It's here – on the floor.
d) Your name isn't Claire.

Exercise 5

Exercise 7

/ɪə/	/eə/
idea dear beer	chair pair where
here disappear	Mary square

Unit 29

Exercise 3
a) I want a lock.
b) Give me the books, please.
d) Look! A rook!

Exercise 5

The cooking pot is full.

The cook is putting sugar in the cooking pot.

a cook

cookery books

a box of wood

Water is falling on the cook's foot.

Exercise 7
could ✓   shirt ✗   wood ✓   girl ✗   full ✓
would ✓   port ✗   foot ✓   sock ✗   good ✓

Unit 30

Exercise 3
a) D   It says 'pull' on this door.   It says 'pool' on this door.
b) S   Here's the pen. Look! It's on the table.   Here's the pen. Look! It's on the table.
c) S   It says 'pull' on this door.   It says 'pull' on this door.
d) D   Look! Here's the pen. It's on the table.   Luke! Here's the pen. It's on the table.

Exercise 5
Column B contains the sound /uː/
Column C contains the sounds /uː/ and /ʊ/.
Column A contains the sound /ʊ/.

Exercise 7

/ʊ/	/uː/
good look cook	school moon pool
foot	tool afternoon tooth

Unit 31

Exercise 5

time ✓   listen ✗   rest ✓   guitar ✓   castle ✗
night ✓   doctor ✓   whistle ✗   often ✗   (but see Tip box on page 68)

Unit 32

Exercise 1

When you say /t/ you cannot feel any movement in your throat: /t/ is unvoiced.
When you say /d/ you can feel movement (vibrations) in your throat: /d/ is voiced.

Exercise 3

a) Do you like tennis?
b) He can ride well.
c) That's a nice card.
d) It's a white tie.

Exercise 4

1   a hard bed
2   a cold wind
3   an old friend
4   a wide road

Exercise 8

heart   town   dry   had   code   train

Unit 33

Exercise 3

a) S   He's got a new car.   He's got a new car.
b) D   These children can't.   These children count.
c) D   He's got a new car.   He's got a new cow.
d) S   These children count.   These children count.

Exercise 5

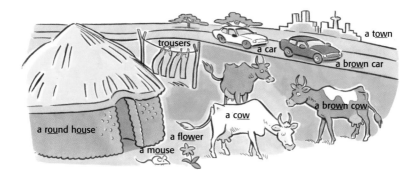

Unit 34

Exercise 3

a) That's my boat.
b) There are two poles here.
c) What a fantastic goal!.
d) Pat's skirt is very nice.

Exercise 5

a) Do you like sewing?
b) It's a large coat.
c) It snores all night.
d) I like all doctors.

Exercise 8

ZOE: Hello Joe!
JOE: Hello Zoe!
ZOE: Where are you going? Are you going home?
JOE: No. I'm going to the mobile phone shop.
ZOE: Oh!
JOE: Where are you going? Are you going home?
ZOE: No. I'm going to the post office.

Exercise 9

know ✓   brown ✗   car ✗   don't ✓   October ✓
work ✗   nose ✓   ball ✗   mouse ✗   joke ✓

Unit 36

Exercise 1

When you say /s/ and /ʃ/ you cannot feel any movement in your throat:

Exercise 3

a) She's very quiet today.
b) There are two shoes here.
c) It's a clean seat.
d) What a dirty shack!

Exercise 6

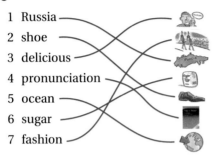

1 Russia
2 shoe
3 delicious
4 pronunciation
5 ocean
6 sugar
7 fashion

Exercise 7

Russia   shoe   delicious   pronunciation   ocean   sugar   fashion

The underlined letters show that you can spell /ʃ/ in six different ways!
But don't worry: the most common is 'sh'. For example: fish, finish, short, shirt

Unit 37

Exercise 1

When you say /ʃ/ you cannot feel any movement in your throat: /ʃ/ is unvoiced.
When you say /ʒ/ you can feel movement (vibrations) in your throat: /ʒ/ is voiced.

Exercise 7

/s/		/ʃ/		/ʒ/	
glass	street	shirt	shopping	measure	
horse		shower	push	pleasure	garage

Unit 38

Exercise 3

a) Those are very large chips
b) I don't like shopping.
c) That's a sheep farm.
d) She's watching the television.

Exercise 7

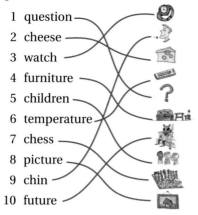

1 question
2 cheese
3 watch
4 furniture
5 children
6 temperature
7 chess
8 picture
9 chin
10 future

ques<u>ti</u>on   <u>ch</u>eese   wat<u>ch</u>   furni<u>t</u>ure   <u>ch</u>ildren   tempera<u>t</u>ure   <u>ch</u>ess   pic<u>t</u>ure   <u>ch</u>in   fu<u>t</u>ure

Exercise 8

/tʃ/ is spelt **with** 'ch'	/tʃ/ is spelt **without** 'ch'
cheese watch	question furniture
children chess chin	temperature picture future

Unit 39

Exercise 1

When you say /tʃ/ you cannot feel any movement in your throat: /tʃ/ is unvoiced.
When you say /dʒ/ you can feel movement (vibrations) in your throat: /dʒ/ is voiced.

Exercise 3

a) Is your name Jerry?
b) I want a cheap type of car.
c) I'm joking.
d) The crowd is jeering.

Exercise 5

1 Everything in the fridge contains the sound /dʒ/.
2 Everything on the kitchen table contains the sound /tʃ/.

Exercise 6

1 Where are the oranges? In the fridge.
2 Where's the chicken? On the kitchen table.
3 Where are the Japanese noodles? In the fridge.
4 Where's the cherry pie? On the kitchen table.
5 Where's the cabbage? In the fridge.
6 Where are the vegetables? In the fridge.
7 Where's the chocolate cake? On the kitchen table.

Exercise 8

/ʃ/	/tʃ/	/dʒ/
shopping Scottish	cheese cheap	jam Joe's
Irish fish sushi	chips spinach	Jerry's Japanese
delicious fresh	Chessington	vegetable cabbage

Unit 40

Exercise 1
When you say /j/ you can feel movement (vibrations) in your throat: /j/ is voiced.

Exercise 3
a) D   Jess, I love you!   Yes, I love you!
b) S   Do you want a jam sandwich?   Do you want a jam sandwich?
c) S   Yes, I love you!   Yes, I love you!
d) D   Do you want a jam sandwich?   Do you want a yam sandwich?

Exercise 4

Exercise 7

Group 1	Group 2	Group 3	Group 4	Group 5
use	(July)	(hello)	(Japan)	new
year	onion	view	few	beautiful
(one)	uniform	student	music	(jam)

Unit 41

Exercise 3
a) Pass me the pepper, please.
b) He's sailing his boat.
c) I've got a bad pain.
d) It's cool in the shade.

Unit 42

Exercise 3
a) Those bees are very noisy.
b) Let's go to the toyshop.
c) Her name's Miss G. Smith.
d) The oil is black.

Exercise 4

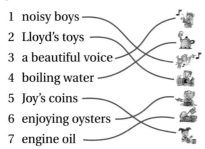

1 noisy boys
2 Lloyd's toys
3 a beautiful voice
4 boiling water
5 Joy's coins
6 enjoying oysters
7 engine oil

Unit 43

Exercise 3
a) His name's Mr. I. Smith
b) What a noisy bike!
c) That boy had a cart.
d) My uncle is a guide.

Exercise 7
MIKE: What are you doing tonight, Clive?
CLIVE: I'm going ice-skating.
MIKE: Have a nice time!
CLIVE: Thanks. Bye!
MIKE: Bye!

Exercise 8

/ɑː/	/aɪ/
garden heart start	height right fight
March artist	bite inside

Unit 44

Exercise 1
When you say /p/ you cannot feel movement in your throat: /p/ is unvoiced.

Exercise 6
picture ✓   photo ✗   pepper ✓   sheep ✓   elephant ✗   cup ✓
Christopher ✗   plate ✓   headphones ✗   phone ✗   potato ✓

Unit 45

Exercise 1
When you say /p/ you cannot feel any movement in your throat: /p/ is unvoiced.
When you say /b/ you can feel movement (vibrations) in your throat: /b/ is voiced.

Exercise 3
a) Have you got a pin?
b) There's a pear in the tree.
c) I don't like bees.
d) I want to get a cab.

Exercise 7

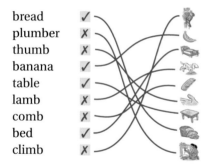

bread   ✓
plumber ✗
thumb   ✗
banana   ✓
table   ✓
lamb   ✗
comb   ✗
bed   ✓
climb   ✗

Unit 46

Exercise 1
When you say /k/ you cannot feel movement in your throat: /k/ is unvoiced.

Exercise 3
DR CLARK: Mr. <u>C</u>ollins, how <u>c</u>an I help you?
MR. COLLINS: Good morning, Do<u>c</u>tor <u>C</u>lark. <u>C</u>an you <u>c</u>ure my heada<u>ch</u>e?
DR CLARK: Oh yes, I <u>c</u>an <u>c</u>ure it with a<u>c</u>upun<u>c</u>ture. <u>C</u>ome ba<u>ck</u> to the <u>c</u>lini<u>c</u> at six
o'clo<u>ck</u>.
MR. COLLINS: Than<u>k</u> you, Do<u>c</u>tor <u>C</u>lark.
DR CLARK: Ta<u>k</u>e <u>c</u>are, Mr. <u>C</u>ollins!

Exercise 4

'c'	'k'	'ck'	'ch'	'x'
coat cat	milk keep king	lock black	school	Taxi fix

Exercise 5

1   I can't walk because my <u>knee</u> hurts.
2   I need a <u>knife</u> to cut the bread.
3   My grandmother loves <u>knitting</u>.
4   I don't <u>know</u> the answer.
5   This <u>doorknob</u> is stuck.
6   There's a big <u>knot</u> in my shoelace.

Unit 47

Exercise 1

When you say /k/ you cannot feel any movement in your throat: /k/ is unvoiced.
When you say /g/ you can feel movement (vibrations) in your throat: /g/ is voiced.

Exercise 3

a)   That's a very small class.
b)   I've got a white coat.
c)   What a lovely little girl!
d)   There's something on your bag.

Exercise 6

eight ✗   ghost ✓   guess ✓   angry ✓   sign ✗
gate ✓   foreign ✗   glue ✓   fight ✗

Track listings

CD A
Track A1 – A98
Duration: 47' 56"

CD B
Track B1 – B93
Duration: 39' 54"

CD C
Track C1 – C99
Duration: 46' 12"